Ancient Greece for Beginners

Greek History Simplified for People Who Slept Through History Class

Free Bonus from Captivating History (Available for a Limited time)

Hi History Lovers!

Now you have a chance to join our exclusive history list so you can get your first history ebook for free as well as discounts and a potential to get more history books for free!

Simply visit the link below to join.

captivatinghistory.com/ebook

Or, Scan the QR code!

Also, make sure to follow us on Facebook, X, and YouTube by searching for Captivating History.

Table of Contents

Introduction
Your Ticket to Ancient Greece

If you're reading this, chances are you either slept through history class or your teacher made ancient Greece sound about as exciting as watching paint dry on an old vase. Maybe you vaguely remember something about the Olympics, or you've seen a movie with men in sandals yelling, "This is Sparta!" Either way, you're here now, and that's what matters.

Here's the truth: ancient Greece is one of the most fascinating, influential, and downright wild periods in human history. Athens developed one of the earliest and most impactful forms of democracy. Greeks wrote plays that still make audiences cry, asked questions that philosophers still can't answer, and built temples that still awe visitors thousands of years later. They were brilliant, brutal, creative, and competitive.

And they shaped everything that came after. When you vote in an election, you're following an ideal of citizen participation inspired in part by Athens. When you go to the theater, thank Athens again. When you use words like "philosophy," "democracy," "chaos," and "marathon" (the name of the battle that inspired the modern race), you're speaking Greek. When you study geometry, biology, or physics, you're following in the footsteps of Greek thinkers who developed methods of logic and reasoning crucial to later scientific advances.

What You'll Discover

This book will take you on a journey spanning over a thousand years, from the Bronze Age rise of the Minoans to the Hellenistic Age's final decline. You'll meet the mysterious Minoans of Crete, the Mycenaean warrior-kings who possibly fought the Trojan War, the Spartans who created a society obsessed with military perfection, and the Athenians who invented democracy and then used it to build an empire.

You'll witness Leonidas and his three hundred Spartans resisting the massive Persian army at Thermopylae. You'll see Greek city-states, including Athens and Sparta, repel two major Persian invasions. You'll watch the philosopher Socrates annoy people by asking questions until they sentenced him to death. You'll follow Alexander the Great as he conquers most of the known world by the age of thirty.

You'll see the birth of the Olympic Games, the construction of the Parthenon, the writing of history's first histories, and Greek thinkers laying early foundations for rational inquiry and empirical observation.

A Note on Honesty

This book won't pretend the Greeks were perfect. They practiced slavery on a massive scale. They denied women basic rights. They could be brutal and arrogant. Athenian democracy only applied to adult male citizens, which was maybe 10 to 20 percent of the population.

We're not going to sugarcoat the uncomfortable parts. The Greeks were real people with real flaws. What made them remarkable wasn't moral perfection; it was their willingness to question, experiment, and push boundaries.

This book also won't drown you in academic jargon or assume you already know who Pericles was. We'll introduce people, places, and concepts as we go.

Let's Begin

We're about to travel back to a world of city-states and citizen-soldiers, of gods and heroes, of philosophers and playwrights. We'll start with the mysterious palace civilization of Crete, journey through the chaos of the Dark Age, watch democracy be born, witness the clash between East and West, and follow Alexander the Great as he conquered the known world from Greece to India.

By the time we're done, you'll understand why this small, mountainous peninsula managed to shape the entire Western world and why we're still talking about it more than two thousand years later.

Welcome to ancient Greece. Let's dive in.

Chapter 1 – Welcome to the Cradle of the West

The Mediterranean Stage: Geography and Climate

If you look at a map of Greece, the first thing you'll notice is how broken up everything is. Mountains everywhere. Hundreds of islands scattered across the sea. Coastline that twists and turns for thousands of miles. This wasn't a landscape that encouraged unity.

The Greek mainland is dominated by mountain ranges that divide the land into small valleys and coastal plains. The Pindus Mountains run like a spine down the western side of the peninsula. Mount Olympus in the north rises to nearly ten thousand feet, so high that the Greeks imagined their gods lived at its peak, above the clouds where mortals couldn't reach.

These mountains meant that ancient Greek communities developed in isolation from each other. A valley might be only thirty miles from the next valley, but the mountain pass between them could be treacherous. Travel was difficult and dangerous, so communities stayed local. They developed their own dialects, customs, gods (though with significant overlap), and eventually governments.

The sea, however, was a different story. Greece has one of the longest coastlines in the Mediterranean relative to its size. No point in Greece is more than about eighty-five miles from the sea. The Aegean Sea, dotted with islands, lies to the east. The Ionian Sea stretches to the west. The Mediterranean opens to the south.

For the Greeks, the sea was a highway. It was far easier to sail from Athens to the island of Delos or even to the coast of Asia Minor (modern-day Turkey) than it was to walk to Thebes, which was only thirty miles away but required crossing mountains. Greek ships could hug the coastline, hopping from island to island, connecting communities across the water in ways that mountains prevented on land.

Because mountains kept communities separate, Greece never became a unified empire like Egypt or Persia. Instead, it developed as hundreds of independent city-states, which the Greeks called a *polis* (plural: *poleis*). Each polis was its own country with its own laws, government, and army. Athens was one polis. Sparta was another. Thebes, Corinth, and Megara are other well-known examples.

Geography wasn't the only reason the city-states remained independent. Greek political philosophy emphasized local autonomy and self-governance. Cultural rivalry between cities was fierce, as each *polis* took pride in its own identity and resisted outside control. The Greeks valued their independence and fought to maintain it, even when unification might have made them stronger against external threats.

But because the sea connected these communities, Greeks shared a common culture despite their political divisions. They spoke variations of the same language. They worshiped the same gods. They competed in the same athletic festivals. They recognized each other as Hellenes, or Greeks, even when they were fighting each other.

The climate also played a role. Greece has a Mediterranean climate. It has hot, dry summers and mild, wet winters. This meant the growing season was limited. The rocky soil wasn't particularly fertile. Ancient Greeks could grow olives, grapes, and some grain, but feeding a large population was always a challenge.

This agricultural limitation had two major effects. First, it encouraged trade. Greeks needed to import grain, so they became seafarers and merchants, trading olive oil, wine, and other goods for the food they needed. Second, it encouraged colonization. When a city's population grew beyond what the land could support, the solution was often to send people overseas to found new colonies.

The landscape also shaped Greek military tactics. In the narrow valleys and mountain passes, large cavalry forces were less effective than in the open plains of Persia or Egypt. Greek warfare evolved around heavily armed foot soldiers known as hoplites who fought in tight formations called phalanxes. The terrain favored defenders. An army holding a mountain pass could stop a much larger force, as the Spartans famously proved at Thermopylae.

So when you think about ancient Greece, don't imagine a unified nation. Imagine a fragmented landscape of independent communities, divided by mountains but connected by the sea, competing with each other constantly but also sharing a common identity. The geography didn't just influence Greek history; it determined it.

The Greeks' View of the World (Hellenes vs. Barbarians)

The ancient Greeks didn't call themselves "Greeks." That's a Latin word that came later. They called themselves Hellenes, and they believed they were fundamentally different from everyone else.

To the Greeks, the world was divided into two types of people: Hellenes and *barbaroi* ("barbarians"). And no, "barbarian" didn't necessarily mean savage or uncivilized, though it sometimes carried that implication. The word *barbaroi* was originally just Greek for "those who speak bar-bar," people whose language sounded like meaningless babbling to Greek ears.

What made someone a Hellene? It wasn't about which city-state you belonged to. A person from Athens and a person from Sparta might be bitter enemies, but they were both Hellenes. Greekness was cultural and ethnic, not political.

Being a Hellene meant you spoke Greek. The language had dialects, like Doric, Ionic, and Aeolic, but they were mutually understandable. You would also participate in Greek religious practices. You worshiped the Olympian gods: Zeus, Hera, Athena, Apollo, and the rest. You attended the great religious festivals like the Olympics or the games at Delphi. Hellenes shared a cultural heritage. You knew the stories of Homer (the *Iliad* and the *Odyssey*). You knew the myths and legends that every Greek child learned.

But here's something crucial to understand. Being a Hellene didn't mean you could become a citizen anywhere in the Greek world. Citizenship was different in each polis. In Athens, for example, citizenship required that both your parents were Athenian citizens. Foreigners who lived in Athens for generations, called *metics,* could be culturally Greek, speak the language perfectly, and worship the same gods, but they could never become full citizens, no matter how long they stayed or how much they contributed to the city. Cultural identity and legal citizenship were two separate things.

Non-Greeks (*barbaroi*) included the Persians, who built the largest empire the world had yet seen. It included the Egyptians, whose civilization was already ancient when Greece was just getting started. The distinction wasn't primarily about sophistication or power; it was more about culture and identity.

The Greeks were aware that other peoples had impressive civilizations. They respected Egyptian knowledge, especially in mathematics and medicine. They recognized Persian military might. However, they still saw themselves as different and, in important ways, superior. Free Greeks governed themselves through assemblies and councils. Barbarians, in the Greek view, bowed to kings and emperors. Greeks valued reason and debate. Barbarians simply obeyed.

This distinction became particularly important during the Persian Wars, when the Greeks framed their conflict as a struggle between freedom and slavery, between the Greek way of life and Persian despotism. Whether this was fair to the Persians is debatable, as Persian society was more complex than Greek propaganda suggested, but it's how the Greeks understood their world.

But here's something interesting: Greek culture was remarkably inclusive in one specific way. When Greeks established colonies around the Mediterranean, they brought their culture with them. People in these colonies, even if they had mixed heritage, could be Hellenes if they adopted the Greek language, religion, and customs. Later, after Alexander the Great's conquests, Greek culture spread even farther, and the boundaries of who could be considered "Greek" became more fluid.

The Hellene barbarian distinction shaped how Greeks saw themselves and their place in the world. It gave them a sense of common identity even when they fought each other. It also gave them a sense of mission. They sought to preserve Greek culture and Greek freedom against the massive empires that surrounded them.

This worldview had its problems. It could lead to arrogance and cultural blindness. But it also helped create a civilization that valued questioning, debate, and individual excellence in ways that few ancient cultures did.

A Quick Map of Time: The Major Eras

Ancient Greek history spans roughly 1,500 years, from around 1600 BCE to 146 BCE. That's an enormous stretch of time. To put it in perspective, that's about as long as the period from the fall of Rome to today. So when we talk about "ancient Greece," we're not talking about one static civilization. We're talking about a culture that rose, peaked, transformed, and eventually merged into something else.

Historians break this long period into several major eras. Think of these as chapters in a much longer story.

The Bronze Age (c. 3000–1100 BCE)

Before there was classical Greece—before Athens, before Sparta, before democracy—there were the Bronze Age civilizations of the Aegean. These were the Minoans on Crete and the Mycenaeans on the Greek mainland.

The Minoans built elaborate palaces and dominated the sea trade. The Mycenaeans built fortress cities and fought wars. These people spoke an early form of Greek and created the world that Homer would later write about in his epics. They're important because they laid the foundation for everything that came after.

But around 1200 BCE, this Bronze Age world collapsed. Cities were destroyed, palaces burned, trade networks broke down, and writing disappeared. What caused this collapse is still debated. It was probably a combination of invasions, natural disasters, and internal upheaval. What matters is that the lights went out across the eastern Mediterranean, and Greece entered a dark age.

The Dark Age (c. 1100–800 BCE)

The period after the Bronze Age collapse is called the Greek Dark Age, and the name fits. Archaeological evidence shows that populations declined dramatically. People abandoned large settlements and retreated to small, isolated villages. Writing disappeared. Trade nearly stopped. It was a period of poverty and isolation.

However, the Dark Age wasn't completely dark. Greek-speaking peoples migrated and settled across the Aegean region. Oral traditions kept stories and legends alive. Gradually, communities began to recover and reorganize. By the end of this period, the foundations for the classical Greek world were being laid.

The Archaic Period (c. 800–500 BCE)

This is when Greece truly begins to take the shape we recognize. Writing returned; it was borrowed and adapted from the Phoenicians. The population grew, and trade resumed. The polis (the independent city-state) emerged as the fundamental unit of Greek political organization.

This was an era of innovation and expansion. Greeks colonized the Mediterranean, founding new cities from Spain to the Black Sea. They experimented with different forms of government. Art and architecture flourished. The first Olympic Games were held in 776 BCE. Homer's epics were written down. Philosophy began with thinkers who asked fundamental questions about the nature of reality.

By the end of the Archaic period, Athens was moving toward democracy, and Sparta had developed its unique military society. The stage was set for Greece's moment in the spotlight.

The Classical Period (c. 500–323 BCE)

This is the Greece most people think of. The Persian Wars united the Greeks against a common enemy and launched Athens to preeminence. The city entered its Golden Age under Pericles, building the Parthenon and becoming a center of culture, philosophy, and drama.

Socrates walked the streets of Athens, questioning everything. His student, Plato, founded his Academy. Playwrights like Sophocles and Euripides created tragedies that audiences still perform today. Herodotus and Thucydides invented the writing of history as we know it.

However, this glorious period was also marked by conflict. The Peloponnesian War between Athens and Sparta tore Greece apart for twenty-seven years, ending with Athens's defeat and the beginning of Sparta's brief supremacy. After Sparta came Thebes. After Thebes came Macedon under Philip II, who conquered the Greek city-states and ended their independence.

Philip's son, Alexander the Great, then conquered the Persian Empire and spread Greek culture across the known world. His death in 323 BCE marks the end of the Classical period and the beginning of something new.

The Hellenistic Period (323–146 BCE)

After Alexander died, his generals carved up his empire into kingdoms—the Ptolemies in Egypt, the Seleucids in Asia, the Antigonids in Macedon. These weren't traditional Greek city-states anymore. They were territorial monarchies ruling diverse populations.

But Greek culture (Hellenistic culture) dominated from the Mediterranean to India. Greek became the international language of commerce and learning. Alexandria in Egypt became the intellectual capital of the world, home to the famous Great Library and Mouseion. Science and mathematics flourished. Philosophy evolved into new schools, like Stoicism and Epicureanism.

The Hellenistic period ended gradually as Rome conquered the Greek east. The final blow to Greek political independence came in 146 BCE when Rome destroyed Corinth and made Greece a province. However, Hellenistic culture itself continued to flourish, especially in Egypt under the Ptolemies, until 30 BCE, when Rome annexed Egypt after the defeat of Cleopatra and Mark Antony. But in a real sense, Greek culture never died. It simply transformed, influencing Rome and, through Rome, all of Western civilization.

Understanding these periods helps make sense of the story we're about to tell. Ancient Greece wasn't one thing. It was a culture that evolved, adapted, achieved greatness, declined, and ultimately survived by transforming itself and influencing everything that came after.

Now let's go back to the beginning and meet the people who started it all.

Chapter 2 – Lost Worlds: The Bronze Foundations and the Dark Age

The Sea Kings of Crete: The Minoan Civilization

Long before there was Athens or Sparta, before Homer sang of heroes, before anyone called themselves Hellenes, there was Crete. On Crete, there was a civilization so sophisticated that when archaeologists first discovered it in the early 1900s, they could hardly believe what they had found.

The Minoans, named after the legendary King Minos, built the first great civilization in Europe. From roughly 2700 to 1450 BCE, they played a dominant role in Aegean maritime trade from their island stronghold. Their palaces were architectural marvels. Their art was vibrant and naturalistic. Their ships connected Mediterranean trade routes. And then, suddenly, they vanished.

The center of Minoan civilization was Knossos, a sprawling palace complex on the northern coast of Crete. Calling it a "palace" doesn't quite capture what it was. Knossos covered about six acres and had hundreds of rooms spread across multiple stories. It had indoor plumbing with running water and sophisticated drainage systems. It had storage rooms that could hold enough food to feed thousands. It had workshops for craftsmen, religious shrines, administrative offices, and residential quarters.

What Knossos didn't have were defensive walls.

This is striking. Most Bronze Age palaces were fortresses. The Mycenaeans on the mainland built massive stone walls around their cities. The Hittites in Anatolia fortified everything. But Knossos and other Minoan palaces on Crete were wide open. There were no walls or obvious military defenses.

The remains of the Palace of Knossos.[1]

This suggests the Minoans felt secure, though the absence of walls doesn't prove they were peaceful. Some scholars argue that their security stemmed from their naval power. Their ships controlled the seas so effectively that no one dared attack the island. Others point to Crete's geographic isolation. The evidence suggests that Minoan ships played a crucial role in Aegean trade, so it is possible they weren't a militant society. Whether through naval strength, isolation, or a genuinely less militaristic culture, the Minoans didn't feel the need to fortify their palaces the way other Bronze Age peoples did.

The palace at Knossos was a maze of corridors, stairways, and rooms. It's easy to see how this place might have inspired the later Greek legend of the Labyrinth–the impossible maze where King Minos imprisoned the Minotaur, a half-man, half-bull monster. The myth says the hero Theseus navigated the Labyrinth, killed the Minotaur, and escaped using a thread given to him by Minos's daughter Ariadne.

Bulls were certainly important to the Minoans. Palace walls were decorated with frescoes showing young athletes performing death-defying acrobatics, vaulting over charging bulls, grabbing their horns, and somersaulting over their backs. Whether this was sport, ritual, or both is unclear. But it was dangerous, and it was central to Minoan culture.

Bull-leaping fresco at the Palace of Knossos.[3]

Minoan art is distinctive. Unlike the rigid, formal art of Egypt or Mesopotamia, Minoan frescoes are fluid and lively. They show dolphins leaping through waves, women in elaborate dresses, flowers and plants, and religious processions. They used bright blues, reds, and yellows. The figures move naturally. There's a joy to Minoan art that you don't often see in the ancient world.

Women appear prominently in Minoan art and might have held significant roles in religious and ritual life, though their actual social and political status remains debated among scholars. Frescoes show women participating in religious ceremonies, overseeing rituals, and engaging in public activities. Some scholars believe Minoans worshiped a mother goddess.

The Minoans were master traders and seafarers. Their pottery has been found throughout the eastern Mediterranean, including in Egypt, on the Greek mainland, in Asia Minor, and on Cyprus. They traded in wine, olive oil, textiles, and luxury goods. They imported tin and copper to make bronze, gold and silver for jewelry, and exotic items from distant lands.

The Minoans were literate and kept detailed records of their palace economies. However, we can't read what they wrote. The earliest Minoan script is called Linear A. It appears on clay tablets found at Knossos and other sites, usually recording inventories and transactions. Scholars have been trying to decipher Linear A for over a century without success. We know it's a syllabic script where each symbol represents a syllable, but we don't know what language it represents. Linguistic analysis suggests it is unrelated to Indo-European languages, meaning it's not Greek or any language family we're familiar with.

Around 1450 BCE, something catastrophic happened to the Minoan civilization. The palaces were destroyed. Some were even burned. Knossos survived, but it came under new management: the Mycenaean Greeks from the mainland. The Minoan culture didn't disappear overnight, but it was never the same.

What caused the collapse? Theories abound. A massive volcanic eruption on the island of Thera (modern Santorini) around 1600 BCE sent tsunamis crashing into Crete and covered parts of the island in volcanic ash. This disaster weakened Minoan power, though the civilization recovered for another century and a half.

Archaeological evidence suggests that around 1450 BCE, Mycenaean Greeks from the mainland established control over Crete. Whether this happened through military conquest, gradual political takeover, or a combination of factors remains debated. What's clear is that after 1450 BCE, Mycenaean Greeks were in charge at Knossos, using Linear B script (an adaptation of Linear A that records Greek) to administer the palace.

The Minoans had created Europe's first great civilization, but they would not be its last. That distinction would belong to the Greeks, who took control of their island.

The Age of Heroes: The Mycenaean Civilization

The Mycenaeans were not like the Minoans. Where the Minoans built unfortified palaces and painted dolphins, the Mycenaeans built fortress cities and buried their kings with weapons. Mycenaean elite culture emphasized warfare and fortifications, suggesting a highly militarized society. These were the Greeks who would become the heroes of legend—Agamemnon, Achilles, and Odysseus. This was the world Homer sang about.

Mycenaean civilization flourished on the Greek mainland from roughly 1600 to 1100 BCE. The name comes from Mycenae, the most powerful of their cities, located in the northeastern Peloponnese. Mycenaean cities dotted the landscape and included Pylos, Tiryns, Athens, Thebes, and Iolkos. Each was an independent kingdom ruled by a *wanax* (similar to a king).

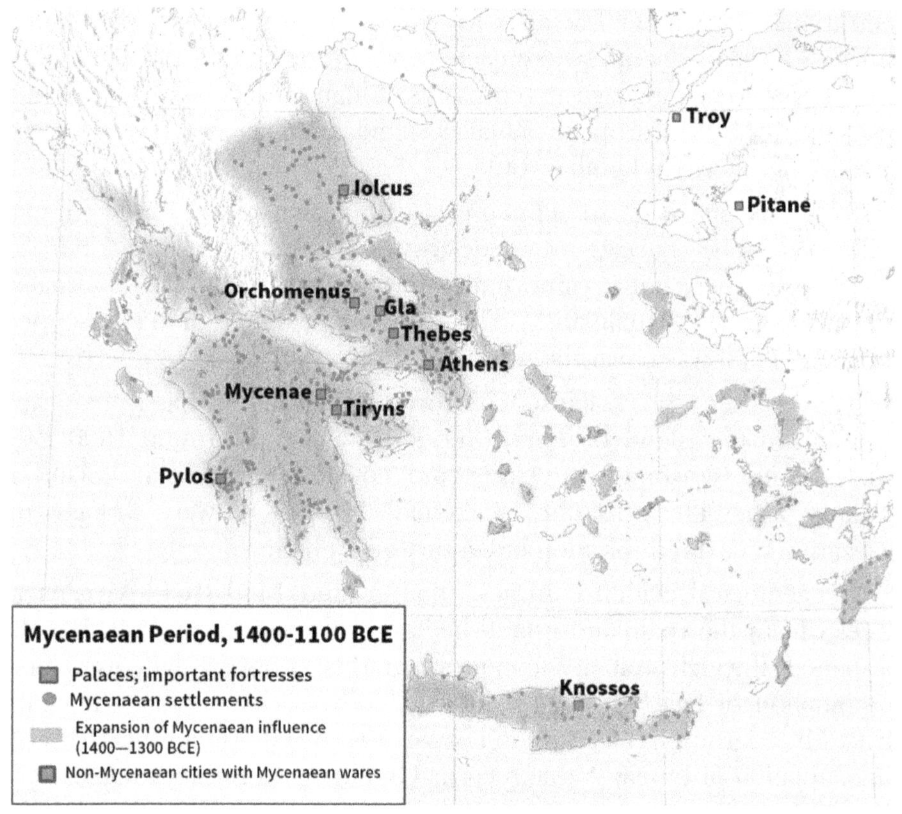

Map of Mycenaean world.[8]

The first thing a person would have noticed about a Mycenaean city was its walls. These weren't simple defensive barriers. They were massive constructions of huge limestone blocks, some weighing several tons, fitted together without mortar. Later Greeks, unable to imagine humans building such things, called them "Cyclopean walls." They imagined they had been built by the mythical one-eyed giants called Cyclopes.

The citadel of Mycenae sits on a hill dominating the Argive Plain. To enter, you pass through the Lion Gate, topped with a relief sculpture of two lions flanking a column. Inside, the citadel contains a palace complex, houses for the elite, storage rooms, workshops, and a secret underground cistern that could provide water during a siege. Everything about Mycenaean architecture suggests they expected an attack and were ready.

The Lion Gate today.[4]

This wasn't paranoia. The Mycenaeans fought each other constantly. Each city-state was independent and competitive. Kings raided each other's territories for cattle, slaves, and glory. War was how Mycenaean elites proved themselves and gained wealth.

According to later Greek tradition preserved in Homer's epics, the Mycenaean kingdoms sometimes united for larger campaigns. The legendary Trojan War would have been such an occasion. Multiple kingdoms supposedly joined under Agamemnon of Mycenae to sail across the Aegean and besiege Troy, a wealthy city on the coast of Asia Minor.

Did the Trojan War really happen? We don't know for certain. There was definitely a city called Troy (or Ilion) where Homer said it was. Archaeologists have found its ruins at Hisarlik in modern Turkey. The site shows evidence of multiple cities built on top of each other, destroyed and rebuilt over centuries. One of these layers, dating to around 1200 BCE, shows signs of destruction by fire and war.

So there was a Troy, and it was destroyed around the right time. But was there really a ten-year siege? Did Agamemnon lead a Greek coalition? Did Achilles kill Hector? Did Odysseus build a wooden horse? We have no evidence of it. What we have is a powerful story that later Greeks believed reflected their ancestral past—a story of heroes, honor, rage, and the terrible costs of war.

What we do know for certain is that Mycenaean Greeks were warriors and sailors. Archaeological evidence shows they engaged in extensive trade throughout the Mediterranean, and they might have conducted raids, though the extent of their military expeditions beyond Greece remains debated. Their pottery has been found as far away as Italy, Egypt, and the Levant. They imported amber from the Baltic, ivory from Syria, and gold from Egypt.

The Mycenaeans also adopted and adapted Minoan practices. After taking control of Crete around 1450 BCE, they assumed control of Minoan trade networks, learned Minoan artistic techniques, and adapted the Minoan Linear A script to write their own language. This adapted script is called Linear B, and unlike Linear A, we can read it.

Linear B was deciphered in 1952 by Michael Ventris, an amateur linguist who proved that the tablets recorded an early form of Greek. The tablets are mostly administrative records, documenting inventories of grain, livestock, textiles, and weapons. They list offerings to the gods, rations for workers, and assignments of land. They're bureaucratic documents, not literature, but they tell us a great deal about how the Mycenaean society functioned.

Mycenaean palaces were administrative centers that controlled the surrounding territory. The king and his bureaucrats tracked everything: how much grain each village produced, how many sheep were raised, how much bronze was available for weapons, how much wool was spun into cloth. This was a literate, organized society with record-keeping and centralized control.

The tablets also reveal aspects of the Mycenaean religion. They mention gods whose names would be familiar to later Greeks, like Zeus, Hera, Poseidon, Hermes, Athena, Artemis, and Dionysus. Some deities known from the later Greek religion appear in Linear B tablets, though their roles and attributes in the Bronze Age might have differed from what we know of the Classical Greek religion. The religious continuity is there, but we shouldn't assume the Bronze Age gods were identical to the Olympians of Homer or later Greek worship.

Mycenaean kings were buried in impressive tombs. At Mycenae, archaeologist Heinrich Schliemann discovered shaft graves containing spectacular grave goods. There were gold masks, bronze weapons inlaid with gold and silver, jewelry, and imported luxury items. One mask, which Schliemann famously (and incorrectly) declared was "the mask of Agamemnon," shows the extraordinary wealth these rulers commanded.

The Mask of Agamemnon.[5]

Later Mycenaean royalty were buried in tholos tombs, massive beehive-shaped chambers dug into hillsides and covered with earth. The Treasury of Atreus at Mycenae has a dome that rises forty-three feet and was the largest unsupported dome in the world until the Romans built the Pantheon over a thousand years later.

But for all their power and sophistication, the Mycenaeans were heading toward catastrophe. Around 1200 BCE, their world would come crashing down.

The Great Collapse: The Bronze Age Mystery

Around 1200 BCE, the eastern Mediterranean world fell apart. It wasn't just Greece. Across the region, great civilizations collapsed almost simultaneously. The Hittite Empire in Anatolia vanished. Egyptian power declined sharply. Cities throughout the Levant were destroyed. Trade networks that had connected the Mediterranean for centuries broke down.

In Greece, the devastation was severe. Mycenaean palaces were burned and abandoned. Pylos was destroyed and never rebuilt. Mycenae itself suffered massive damage. Populations declined dramatically. Archaeological surveys suggest Greece lost up to 90 percent of its population in some regions.

Writing disappeared. The administrative systems that had tracked grain and bronze vanished. The long-distance trade networks collapsed. The specialized craftsmen who made luxury goods were gone. The centralized palace economies that had organized production were finished.

This wasn't just a political collapse. This was a civilizational breakdown.

What caused it? Historians have debated this question for decades and still don't have a definitive answer. The most honest response is probably that several things worked together to create a perfect storm.

One definite factor was warfare. Egyptian records from this period mention invasions by "Sea Peoples"—mysterious raiders from the sea who attacked Egypt, Cyprus, and the Levantine coast. We don't know exactly who these Sea Peoples were. They might have been displaced populations fleeing troubles in their own lands, or they might have been opportunistic raiders taking advantage of growing instability. Either way, they contributed to the chaos.

Climate change likely played a role. Evidence suggests the eastern Mediterranean experienced a prolonged drought during this period. Crops would have failed. Food shortages would have created unrest. Populations would have moved, putting pressure on neighboring regions. Hungry people make desperate decisions.

Earthquakes could have compounded the problems. The Aegean region is seismically active, and archaeological evidence shows that several Mycenaean sites suffered earthquake damage around this time. A major earthquake could destroy a palace and its surrounding town. That means multiple earthquakes over a short period could be catastrophic.

Systems collapse is another possibility. Bronze Age civilizations were interconnected through trade. Making bronze requires copper and tin, which usually came from different regions. If trade routes were disrupted, people couldn't make bronze tools or weapons. If they couldn't make weapons, they couldn't defend themselves. If one civilization collapsed, it could trigger a cascade effect as others lost access to necessary resources.

Internal upheaval probably contributed too. Mycenaean society was hierarchical and controlled from the palace centers. If the king and his bureaucracy lost control, whether through war, natural disaster, or internal rebellion, the whole system could unravel. Without the palace organizing production and redistribution, local economies would collapse.

As we said, the truth is probably all of the above. It was likely a perfect storm of disasters: drought and famine, earthquakes, invasions, trade disruption, and internal breakdown. One problem would have made societies vulnerable to others. The combination was overwhelming.

What's clear is that the world that emerged after 1200 BCE was dramatically different from what came before. The palaces were gone. The kings were gone. The bureaucrats, the scribes, and the specialized craftsmen were all gone. Greece entered a period historians call the Dark Age, and the name is appropriate.

But here's something important to remember. While civilization collapsed at the elite level, people survived. They continued farming, herding, and living in small communities. They told stories about the great heroes of the past, stories that would eventually become the *Iliad* and the *Odyssey.* They remembered the gods, and they spoke Greek.

The Bronze Age world was gone, but Greek culture survived, kept alive in oral traditions through centuries of poverty and isolation. Eventually, slowly, it would begin to rebuild.

The Quiet Centuries: The Greek Dark Age

The period from roughly 1100 to 800 BCE is called the Greek Dark Age, though "quiet centuries" might be more accurate. It wasn't completely dark. People lived, farmed, raised families, and told stories. However, it was a dramatic step backward from the sophistication of the Mycenaean world.

Archaeological evidence from this period is sparse. Settlements were small; they were more like villages than towns. Houses were simple structures of mudbrick and thatch. There were no palaces, no monumental architecture, and no elaborate tombs. Pottery was functional but plain, lacking the artistic sophistication of earlier or later periods.

Most significantly, writing disappeared. The Linear B tablets stop around 1200 BCE, and for the next four hundred years, Greece was illiterate. Knowledge and stories were preserved orally, passed down through generations by memory. Without written records, we know frustratingly little about what happened during these centuries.

The population declined dramatically. Surveys of archaeological sites show that many Mycenaean-era settlements were abandoned. People retreated to defensible hilltop locations or scattered into isolated farmsteads. Greece might have lost 75 to 90 percent of its population in some regions, though exact figures are impossible to determine.

Trade contracted severely. The long-distance maritime networks that had connected Greece to Egypt, the Levant, and Cyprus largely ceased. A few imported items from the Near East still appear in Greek sites, but the flow of goods reduced to a trickle. Greeks became more isolated and more focused on local survival than international commerce.

The political structure changed fundamentally. There were no more palace bureaucracies, no more *wanax* ruling from fortified citadels. Instead, Greece fragmented into small communities led by local chiefs or councils of elders. These were societies where everyone knew everyone else, not the organized kingdoms of the Bronze Age.

But life continued. People grew barley and wheat. They raised sheep and goats. They made pottery for everyday use. They buried their dead, usually in simple graves with few grave goods. They worshiped the gods, though without the elaborate rituals organized by palace priesthoods.

Around 1050 BCE, a new burial practice appeared: cremation. Bodies were burned on funeral pyres, and the ashes were placed in urns. This practice is quite different from earlier inhumation burials and became the standard during much of the Greek Dark Age. Whether this represents a change in religious beliefs or was simply practical is unclear.

During this period, Greeks began migrating across the Aegean to the coast of Asia Minor (modern Turkey). The traditional story, recorded by later Greek historians, says that different Greek tribal groups colonized different regions. Ionians settled the central coast and islands like Samos and Chios. Aeolians moved to the northern coast. Dorians went to the southern coast and islands like Rhodes. These migrations established a Greek presence throughout the Aegean Basin, creating communities that would remain Greek-speaking for thousands of years.

One significant development during the Greek Dark Age was the introduction of iron. Bronze had been the premier metal for tools and weapons throughout the Bronze Age, but iron is more abundant and, once you know how to work it, more practical. Iron ore is much more common than copper and tin. An iron blade can be harder and sharper than bronze.

Iron-working knowledge probably spread to Greece from the Near East or Cyprus around 1050 BCE. By 900 BCE, iron had replaced bronze for most everyday tools and weapons. This democratized access to metal implements. A person no longer needed long-distance trade networks to get the materials for functional tools. This might have contributed to the eventual recovery of Greek society.

Toward the end of the Dark Age, around 900 to 800 BCE, things began to improve. Populations started growing again. Settlements became larger and more prosperous. Pottery grew more sophisticated. Trade connections began to reestablish. The stirrings of recovery were underway.

Songs of Heroes: Homer and the Epic Tradition

Sometime around 750 to 700 BCE, Greek culture produced two poems that would shape Western literature for millennia: the *Iliad* and the *Odyssey*. Attributed to a poet named Homer, these epic poems told stories of heroes, wars, gods, and the human condition with such power that they have never stopped being read.

Whether Homer actually existed as a single person is debated. The poems might have been composed by one brilliant poet, or they might have been the culmination of a long oral tradition, assembled from songs and stories passed down through generations. Ancient Greeks believed Homer was real. They thought he was a blind bard who sang of the Trojan War and its aftermath. Modern scholars are more cautious. What matters is that these poems appeared, in roughly their current form, during the 8th century BCE.

A bust of Homer.[6]

The *Iliad* doesn't tell the whole story of the Trojan War. It focuses on a few weeks during the tenth and final year of the siege of Troy. The plot centers on the rage of Achilles, the greatest Greek warrior, who withdraws from battle after being dishonored by Agamemnon, the Greek commander. Without Achilles, the Greeks suffer terrible losses. His best friend Patroclus borrows Achilles's armor and enters the battle to save the Greeks, but he is killed by Hector, the greatest Trojan warrior. Achilles, mad with grief and rage, returns to the battle, kills Hector in single combat, and desecrates his body.

The poem ends not with Troy's fall but with Hector's funeral. In a powerful final scene, Hector's father, King Priam, comes alone to Achilles's tent to beg for his son's body. Achilles is reminded of his own father and pities him. He returns Hector's body, and the two enemies share a moment of human connection in the midst of war's brutality.

The *Iliad* is about many things: honor, glory, the cost of rage, and the tragedy of war. It shows heroes who are magnificent, petty, brave, and cruel. It shows gods who are immortal but behave like petulant humans, interfering in mortal affairs for their own amusement. It recognizes war's glory—the *kleos* (glory) that warriors sought—while never flinching from its horror.

The *Odyssey* is a different kind of poem. It's an adventure story following Odysseus's ten-year journey home to Ithaca after the fall of Troy. Odysseus faces monsters and witches, including the Cyclops Polyphemus, the enchantress Circe, the Sirens whose song lures sailors to their deaths, the six-headed monster Scylla, and the whirlpool Charybdis. He visits the underworld and meets the shades of dead heroes. He loses all his men through misfortune and their own foolishness.

Meanwhile, back in Ithaca, his wife Penelope fends off suitors who assume Odysseus is dead and want to marry her and take his kingdom. His son, Telemachus, has grown from boy to man during his father's absence. When Odysseus finally returns, disguised as a beggar, he must prove his identity and reclaim his home by slaughtering the suitors with Telemachus's help.

The *Odyssey* celebrates cleverness over strength. Odysseus is *polytropos* ("of many turns," which means he is versatile and cunning). He survives not by being the best fighter (that was Achilles) but by being smart, adaptable, and relentlessly determined to get home. He lies, he tricks, he endures humiliation—whatever it takes to survive and return to his family.

Together, these poems gave Greeks a shared cultural reference point. Every educated Greek knew Homer's stories. Verses from the epics were quoted constantly. Achilles, Hector, and Odysseus became models of different virtues and warnings of different flaws. The poems raised questions. Is glory worth its cost? What makes a good leader? How should we treat enemies? What does it mean to be civilized?

The poems also preserved memories of the Bronze Age world. Homer describes warriors using bronze weapons and fighting from chariots, which were techniques from the Mycenaean era that were obsolete by his own time. He mentions palaces and kingdoms that had vanished centuries earlier. His geography is sometimes confused, combining real places with legendary ones, which suggests these might be cultural memories filtered through generations of oral retelling.

But Homer's poems did more than preserve the past. They defined Greek values and identity. The heroes were flawed humans, not perfect beings. They struggled with anger, pride, fear, and grief—emotions every Greek (and every human) could recognize. The gods were powerful but unpredictable, helping their favorites and punishing those who offended them. Mortals had to navigate a world where you might do everything right and still suffer because some god decided to make your life difficult.

These poems established the epic tradition in Western literature. Every hero's journey, every quest narrative, every story of war and homecoming echoes Homer. Virgil's *Aeneid*, Dante's *Divine Comedy*, Milton's *Paradise Lost*, and Joyce's *Ulysses* all engage with Homer. The *Iliad* and *Odyssey* set the template.

For the Greeks themselves, Homer was education. Boys memorized long passages. The poems taught Greek virtues, like courage, honor, loyalty, hospitality to strangers (*xenia*), and respect for the gods. They taught the Greek language; Homer's poetic dialect became the literary standard. They taught history and mythology, where the Greeks came from, how their world was ordered, and why things were the way they were.

As Greece emerged from the Dark Age into the Archaic period, Homer's poems provided cultural unity. Greeks across hundreds of independent city-states, speaking different dialects and following different governments, could all claim these heroes as their ancestors, these gods as their pantheon, and these values as their inheritance. The poems helped define what it meant to be Greek.

From these foundations—the Minoan palaces, the Mycenaean fortresses, the survival through dark centuries, and the songs of Homer—classical Greek civilization would arise. The stage was set for the next act: the birth of the polis and the Archaic revolution that would transform Greece forever.

Chapter 3 – The Archaic Revolution: Birth of the City-State

A Community of Citizens: The Birth of the Polis

Around 800 BCE, something new began to emerge from the ruins of the Greek Dark Age. Populations were growing. Trade was returning. And Greeks were creating a new form of political organization that would define their civilization for the next five hundred years: the polis.

The word polis is usually translated as "city-state," but that translation doesn't quite capture what it meant. A polis wasn't just a city with surrounding territory. It was a community of citizens, a political entity where members shared identity, governance, and mutual obligations. The polis was the center of Greek life, loyalty, and identity.

Each polis was typically independent and sovereign. It had its own laws, its own government, its own army, its own coinage, and its own calendar. Athens was a polis. So were Sparta, Thebes, Corinth, Megara, and hundreds of others. Some were large and powerful, controlling substantial territory. Others were tiny, perhaps just a town and a few surrounding villages. But each considered itself an autonomous political community, though in practice some smaller settlements remained subordinate to larger neighbors.

The physical layout of most major poleis followed a similar pattern, though this varied considerably in smaller or earlier settlements. At the center was the acropolis (literally "high city"), a defensible hill that served as a refuge in times of war and as a sacred space for temples. The most famous acropolis is in Athens, crowned by the Parthenon (built in the 5th century BCE, well after the Archaic period), but many poleis had one.

Ruins of the Temple of Apollo in Corinth. The city's acropolis can be seen in the background.[7]

Below the acropolis lay the town itself, and at its heart was the agora, which was the marketplace and public square. The agora was where citizens gathered to buy and sell goods, but it was much more than a market. It was where people met to discuss politics, where orators gave speeches, philosophers taught, and news was shared. The agora was the social and political heart of the polis.

Around the town, farmland stretched out–the chora. Most citizens of a polis were farmers who lived in the surrounding countryside and came to town for festivals, assemblies, and market days.

What made someone a citizen? This varied by polis, but citizenship always meant more than just living somewhere. It was a legal status that brought both rights and responsibilities. Citizens could participate in political assemblies, vote on laws, hold office, and own land. In return, they were expected to fight in the army when called, contribute financially to the state, and participate in religious festivals and civic life.

Citizenship was exclusive. In most poleis, only adult males born to citizen parents could be citizens. Women, foreigners (even those born in the city), and slaves had no political rights. In Athens, citizenship would eventually require that both parents were Athenian citizens. This meant citizenship was hereditary and jealously guarded. A polis wasn't an open community that anyone could join; it was a closed club of citizens who shared common ancestry and identity.

This exclusivity created a strong sense of belonging among citizens. You weren't just living in a polis. You were part of it, invested in it, and responsible for it. The polis belonged to its citizens collectively, and they governed it together through assemblies, councils, and magistrates. The specific form of government varied—some poleis were oligarchies ruled by wealthy elites, others developed democracy, a few retained kings—but the principle remained: citizens governed themselves.

The polis also had religious significance. Each polis had patron gods and goddesses who protected it and received worship at civic festivals. Athens had Athena. Sparta had Artemis and Apollo. Corinth had Aphrodite. These weren't just private religious beliefs. Civic religion was part of what bound citizens together. Participating in religious festivals was a civic duty, and impiety toward the city's gods could be punished.

Why did the polis develop this way? Geography played a role. The mountainous terrain of Greece encouraged small, independent communities rather than large centralized kingdoms. The polis was also a political choice, a way of organizing society that emphasized local control, citizen participation, and communal identity.

The development of the polis marked a significant shift from Bronze Age political structures. The Mycenaean *wanax* and their palace bureaucracies were gone. In their place came communities where citizens, at least those with citizenship status, had a voice in governance. This wasn't democracy yet in most places, but it was a step toward the idea that political power came from the citizen body rather than from hereditary monarchs. That said, important continuities remained, including religious practices, regional identities, and certain elite traditions that connected the polis system to earlier Greek culture.

The emergence of the polis around 800 to 700 BCE set the template for Greek political life. For the next several centuries, the polis would be the fundamental unit of Greek civilization. Greeks didn't think of themselves as subjects of a king or empire; they thought of themselves as citizens of their polis. Your polis was your identity, your loyalty, your home. Greeks would fight and die for their polis. They would also refuse to surrender their independence even when unification might have made them stronger.

This intense local patriotism had consequences. Greece would remain politically fragmented, with hundreds of independent poleis competing and often warring with each other. But this fragmentation also created diversity and experimentation. Different poleis tried different forms of government, different social systems, and different economic strategies. Some succeeded, while some failed. However, the competition and variety generated innovation and energy that propelled Greek culture forward.

The polis wasn't perfect. Its exclusion of women, foreigners, and slaves from citizenship was a huge limitation. Its fierce independence prevented Greek unity and left the poleis vulnerable to external threats. But the polis created communities where citizens participated in their own governance, debated policy, and took collective responsibility for their society. This was the foundation on which classical Greek civilization would be built.

From Kings to Oligarchs: Early Governance

In the early Archaic period, most poleis transitioned away from a monarchy toward rule by aristocratic elites—a system called oligarchy, literally "rule by the few." This transition was gradual and varied by location, but the pattern was common throughout Greece.

The Mycenaean kingdoms had been ruled by *wanax* (kings), who controlled palace economies through extensive bureaucracies. When the Bronze Age collapsed, these centralized kingdoms disappeared. During the Greek Dark Age, local leaders—*basileis* in Greek, often translated as "kings" but really meaning something closer to "chiefs"—held authority in small communities. These *basileis* were primarily war leaders and judges, not absolute monarchs.

As poleis developed, power shifted from individual *basileis* to councils of aristocrats, the *aristoi*, meaning "the best people." These were landholding families who claimed descent from the heroes of old. They owned the best farmland, commanded the most retainers, and formed the social and military elite of the polis's army. Their wealth, military importance, and noble lineage gave them political dominance.

In many poleis, aristocratic councils gradually superseded or eliminated kingship altogether. Athens provides a clear example. According to tradition, Athens had kings in the distant past, but by the 7th century BCE, power had passed to nine annually elected magistrates called archons, all drawn from aristocratic families. These archons handled military, religious, and judicial affairs. After their year in office, they became members of the Areopagus, a council of ex-archons that held a lot of power.

Sparta kept its monarchy, but there was an unusual twist. Two kings from different families ruled at the same time. Their power was limited by a council of elders (the Gerousia) and annually elected magistrates (the ephors). Spartan kingship was hedged with so many restrictions that it was hardly absolute rule.

In other poleis, oligarchies governed through councils restricted to wealthy citizens. In Corinth, the Bacchiad family ruled as an oligarchy for nearly a century, with only family members eligible for office. In Thebes, political power rested with a select group of wealthy landowners.

This oligarchic system created social tensions. The aristocrats held most of the land, most of the wealth, and all the political power. They formed the social and military elite, though in Greek terrain, cavalry forces were limited compared to other regions. Below them were ordinary citizens, like the small farmers, craftsmen, and traders, who had citizenship status and military obligations but limited political voice. Below them were non-citizens and slaves who had no voice at all.

Conflicts arose over several issues. Land ownership was a constant problem. Aristocrats accumulated land while small farmers struggled. When farmers fell into debt, they risked losing their land or even their freedom. In some places, debtors could be enslaved or forced to work as tenant farmers on land they once owned.

Legal disputes also favored the wealthy. In early Archaic Greece, laws were unwritten and administered by aristocratic magistrates who could interpret them however they wished. If you were a poor farmer bringing a case against a wealthy landowner, you had little hope of fair treatment.

Military changes intensified these tensions. In the early Archaic period, aristocratic champions and individual warriors played prominent roles in battles, much as Homeric heroes did. But gradually, a new military formation emerged: the phalanx, made up of heavily armed infantrymen called hoplites.

A hoplite carried a large round shield, a spear, and wore bronze armor. In battle, hoplites fought in tight formation, with their shields overlapping and their spears pointed forward. The phalanx was devastatingly effective. A disciplined formation of hoplites could defeat larger numbers of less organized troops.

A hoplite, c. 500 BCE.[8]

Hoplites weren't exclusively aristocrats. They were citizens wealthy enough to afford armor, which included prosperous farmers, successful craftsmen, and traders. These men now formed the backbone of many poleis' military power. They fought in the phalanx, risked their lives defending the polis, and, some historians argue, increasingly demanded political rights equal to their military importance. However, the direct connection between hoplite warfare and political reform remains debated among scholars. The relationship was likely more complex and varied across different poleis than a simple cause-and-effect.

This created pressure on the oligarchic system. If you're expected to fight and die for the polis, shouldn't you have a say in how it's governed? If the polis depends on hoplites for defense, shouldn't hoplites have political representation?

Different poleis responded differently to these pressures. Some oligarchies resisted change and maintained exclusive rule. Others gradually expanded political participation, allowing more citizens into assemblies and magistracies. Still others experienced violent upheaval as tensions boiled over into conflict.

One response to these social tensions was the written law code. Putting laws in writing and displaying them publicly limited aristocratic judges' ability to manipulate the legal system. Everyone could see what the law said. This didn't create equality, as the rich still had advantages, but it was a step toward transparency and accountability.

These tensions also sometimes led to reform, as in Athens, where leaders like Solon would attempt to address grievances through legislation. Sometimes they would lead to tyranny, as ambitious individuals seized power by championing popular causes against the oligarchs. And sometimes they would lead to revolution, as citizens overthrew exclusive oligarchies and established broader participation.

The transition from kingship to oligarchy wasn't the end of Greece's political evolution; it was just one step in a longer journey toward various forms of citizen governance.

Hungry for Land: The Age of Colonization

Between roughly 750 and 550 BCE, Greeks spread across the Mediterranean and Black Sea in one of the most dramatic expansions in ancient history. They founded hundreds of new colonies from Spain to the coast of modern Ukraine and from southern France to North Africa. This Greek colonization movement transformed the Mediterranean world and spread Greek culture far beyond the Greek homeland.

Why did the Greeks leave home? The motivations were diverse and complex. Population pressure was one significant factor. During the Greek Dark Age, populations had declined dramatically. But by the 8th century BCE, recovery was underway. Populations grew, and Greece's rocky soil couldn't support everyone. Farmland was limited, and the best land was already owned by aristocratic families. Younger sons with no prospect of inheriting land faced grim choices: scrape by as landless laborers or seek opportunities elsewhere.

But the need for farmable land wasn't the only motivation. Political conflict drove many emigrants. When rival factions fought for control of a polis, the losers often left rather than face persecution. Exiles needed somewhere to go. Colonization offered a solution.

Trade opportunities attracted others. As long-distance commerce recovered, merchants identified promising locations for trading posts—places where Greek goods could be exchanged for grain, metals, slaves, and other commodities. Colonies could serve as permanent trading stations, facilitating commerce and generating wealth. Some individuals sought adventure or escape from debt or legal troubles.

Some colonies were founded by official expeditions organized by a mother city (*metropolis* in Greek). The mother city would appoint a founder (*oikist*) to lead colonists to a predetermined location. The colonists would establish a new polis, complete with an agora, temples, and farmland divided among settlers. While new colonies were generally politically independent (*apoikia*), they typically maintained religious and sentimental ties with their mother cities. Some retained closer economic or political connections than others.

Other colonies developed more informally, as traders established settlements that gradually grew into permanent communities. Pirates and adventurers also founded settlements in promising locations. The colonization process differed greatly, reflecting the disunited nature of the Greek world.

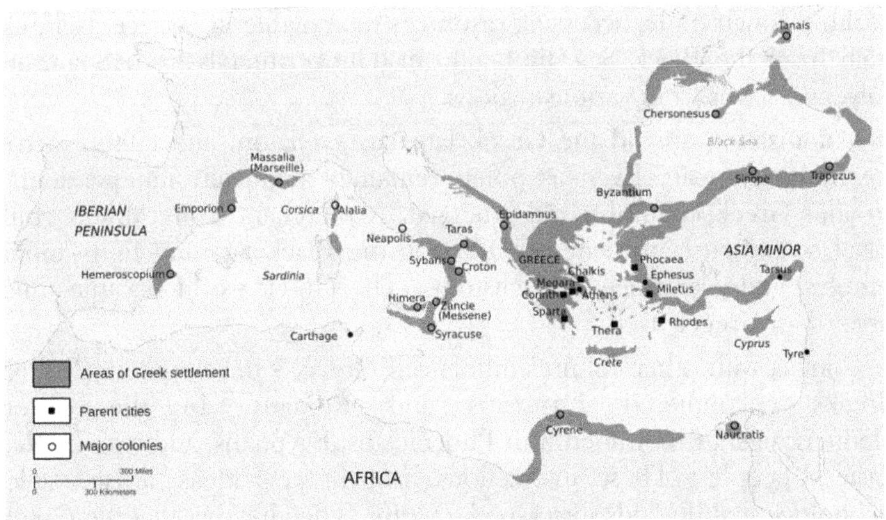

Greek colonies in the Archaic period.[9]

Greek colonies spread in all directions. To the west, Greeks colonized southern Italy and Sicily in such numbers that the region became known as Magna Graecia ("Greater Greece"). Cities like Syracuse, Tarentum, and Neapolis (modern Naples) were founded during this period. Syracuse, founded by the Corinthians around 733 BCE, would become one of the most powerful Greek cities anywhere.

Farther west, Greeks reached southern France, founding Massalia (modern Marseille) around 600 BCE. They even established colonies on the eastern coast of Spain. Greeks were settling the western Mediterranean, competing and trading with Phoenicians who were doing the same from the opposite direction.

To the north and northeast, Greeks colonized the coast of Thrace and the shores of the Black Sea. Cities like Byzantium (later Constantinople, now Istanbul) controlled strategic locations on trade routes. Black Sea colonies could access the grain-rich regions of what is now Ukraine and southern Russia, importing vast quantities of wheat back to Greece.

To the south, Greeks established colonies in North Africa. Cyrene, founded around 630 BCE in what is now Libya, became wealthy from agriculture and the export of silphium, a valuable medicinal plant. Egypt, while not colonized by the Greeks, saw Greek traders establish a permanent trading post at Naucratis in the Nile Delta.

These colonies transformed Greek civilization. They helped ease land pressures by providing farmland for landless Greeks. They generated wealth through trade, accessing resources unavailable in Greece itself, like grain from the Black Sea, timber from Thrace, metals from Spain and Italy, and slaves from various regions.

Colonization spread the Greek language, religion, and culture across the Mediterranean. Even as poleis remained politically independent, a broader Greek cultural world emerged. A merchant from Athens could travel to Syracuse in Sicily or Olbia on the Black Sea and find familiar temples, gods, language, and customs. The Greek world became much larger than Greece itself.

Contact with other cultures influenced Greece's development. In Italy, Greeks encountered Etruscans and Romans. In the eastern Mediterranean, they traded with Phoenicians, Egyptians, and various Near Eastern peoples. These interactions brought new ideas, artistic styles, technologies, and goods into Greek culture. The alphabet that the Greeks adopted from the Phoenicians enabled the return of literacy. Artistic motifs from Egypt and the Near East influenced Greek art. Military tactics learned from various peoples improved Greek warfare.

Colonization also intensified competition among Greek poleis. Mother cities competed to establish colonies in strategic locations. Colonies competed with each other for territory and trade advantages. This competition drove innovation and ambition, but it also created conflicts. Wars between Greek colonies or between colonies and native populations were common.

The native peoples Greeks encountered had varied experiences with Greek colonization. Sometimes, Greeks established colonies in sparsely populated areas with minimal conflict. Sometimes, they displaced existing populations through force. Often, they engaged in trade and cultural exchange with neighboring peoples, sometimes leading to intermarriage and cultural blending. The Greeks generally considered non-Greeks (*barbaroi*) inferior, but practical considerations often led to cooperation and coexistence.

By 550 BCE, the age of widespread colonization was winding down. The most desirable locations had been settled. Existing colonies consolidated their territories rather than found new settlements. However, the impact was permanent. The Mediterranean had become, in significant ways, a Greek sea, though Phoenicians (and their Carthaginian colonies), Etruscans, and other peoples continued to control substantial regions. Greek culture, trade, and political models influenced areas far from mainland Greece.

The age of colonization was one of the most consequential developments in Greek history. It eased social pressures in mainland Greece, generated wealth through expanded trade, spread Greek culture far and wide, and created a huge network of independent Greek cities connected by language, religion, and culture despite political fragmentation.

The Rise of the Strongman: Tyranny

As social tensions increased in many poleis during the 7th and 6th centuries BCE, a new political phenomenon emerged: the tyrant. In Greek, a *tyrannos* was someone who seized power outside the traditional constitutional framework. This person was not necessarily cruel or oppressive (though some certainly were), but he was a person who ruled without legal authority, often by popular support and military force.

The Greek concept of tyranny is important to understand because it differs from the modern meaning. Today, "tyrant" means a brutal dictator. In ancient Greece, it simply meant someone who took power unconstitutionally. Many Greek tyrants were popular reformers who improved their cities. Others were oppressive. The term described how they gained power, not necessarily how they used it.

Tyrants typically emerged from the aristocracy but positioned themselves as champions of ordinary citizens against the oligarchic establishment. The pattern was common. An ambitious aristocrat would recognize popular grievances, such as land distribution, debt burdens, or exclusion from political power, and use these issues to build support. With backing from discontented citizens and perhaps a personal armed force, he would seize control of the polis, overthrowing or sidelining the oligarchic government.

Once in power, tyrants often enacted popular reforms. They redistributed land seized from political enemies, providing farms to landless citizens. They reduced or canceled debts, easing burdens on poor farmers. They sponsored public works projects, such as temples, fortifications, and water systems, creating employment and enhancing the city's prestige. They promoted trade and manufacturing, which benefited merchants and craftsmen. These policies made tyrants popular with ordinary citizens even as they enraged the dispossessed aristocrats.

Tyranny appeared across the Greek world, but it was particularly common in wealthy commercial poleis. Corinth provides a classic example. Around 657 BCE, Cypselus overthrew the Bacchiad oligarchy that had ruled Corinth for decades. The Bacchiads were an aristocratic clan that monopolized power and wealth. Cypselus, who came from a Bacchiad family himself, positioned himself as a champion of excluded citizens. After seizing power, he ruled for about thirty years and was followed by his son, Periander, who ruled for another forty years. Under the Cypselid tyranny, Corinth became one of Greece's most prosperous and powerful cities, dominating trade and founding colonies.

Sicyon, Megara, Athens, Miletus, and many other poleis experienced tyranny during the Archaic period. Some tyrannies lasted decades, while others collapsed quickly. But the phenomenon was widespread enough to be recognized as a distinct stage in Greek political development. It was a transitional stage between an exclusive oligarchy and broader forms of government.

Tyrants maintained power through various means. Popular support was crucial. As long as the majority of citizens benefited from the tyrant's rule, they would tolerate or support his unconstitutional position. Military force mattered too. Tyrants often maintained bodyguards and controlled the city's armed forces. Building projects and festivals kept people employed and entertained. Alliances with other tyrants or foreign powers provided external support.

However, tyranny had weaknesses. It depended on the individual tyrant's ability and popularity. A capable, popular tyrant could rule successfully for decades, but his sons often lacked his qualities. The second or third generation of a tyrannical dynasty typically proved less competent, more oppressive, or simply less necessary. Once the original grievances that brought the tyrant to power were addressed, citizens questioned why they should tolerate unconstitutional rule.

Opposition came from multiple directions. Dispossessed aristocrats schemed constantly to regain power, sometimes calling on Sparta, which opposed tyranny in principle, for help. Citizens who initially supported the tyrant might turn against him if his rule became oppressive or if his reforms succeeded so well that his continued rule seemed unnecessary. Rival ambitious men might attempt their own coups.

Most tyrannies eventually fell. Some were overthrown by aristocratic factions, others by popular uprisings, and still others by foreign intervention. In Athens, the Peisistratid tyranny (which we'll examine in detail in the next chapter) was overthrown in 510 BCE with Spartan help. In Corinth, the Cypselids were eventually expelled.

What did tyranny accomplish? In the short term, tyrants addressed social tensions that oligarchies couldn't or wouldn't resolve. They broke the stranglehold of exclusive aristocratic rule. They demonstrated that power didn't have to reside solely in hereditary noble families. They also promoted economic development and civic pride through building projects and support for trade.

In the longer term, tyranny helped pave the way for democracy in some poleis. By weakening aristocratic power and demonstrating that non-aristocrats could govern effectively, tyrants showed that political participation could be broadened. Once tyranny ended, some poleis—most famously Athens—established democratic systems that gave political rights to broad classes of citizens. Other poleis returned to an oligarchy or mixed constitutions, but even these were usually less exclusively aristocratic than before.

The age of tyranny was largely over by the end of the 6th century BCE. Later Greek political thought would view tyranny negatively, as an illegitimate seizure of power that destroyed constitutional government. But in the Archaic period, tyranny disrupted rigid oligarchies and allowed for political innovation and social reform that might not have occurred otherwise.

Finding the Voice: The Invention of the Alphabet

One of the most important developments of the Archaic period occurred around 800 to 750 BCE. Greeks adopted and adapted an alphabetic writing system from the Phoenicians. This return of literacy after four centuries would transform Greek civilization, enabling everything from written law codes to philosophy to the recording of epic poetry.

The Mycenaeans had been literate, using Linear B to record palace administration. But when the Bronze Age collapsed around 1200 BCE, writing disappeared. For four hundred years, Greece was illiterate. Knowledge, stories, and traditions were preserved orally, passed down through memory and performance. This worked well enough, but oral culture has limitations. Complex information is difficult to preserve accurately across generations. Administrative organization requiring detailed record-keeping becomes nearly impossible.

The return of writing changed everything. Greeks adapted the alphabetic writing system from the Phoenicians, seafaring traders from the Levantine coast (modern Lebanon) who had developed an efficient consonantal script. The Phoenician alphabet used about twenty-two symbols, each representing a consonant sound. It was simpler and more flexible than earlier writing systems, like Egyptian hieroglyphics or Mesopotamian cuneiform, which used hundreds of symbols.

Greeks made a crucial innovation, though. They added vowel symbols to the Phoenician alphabet. Phoenician writing represented only consonants, so readers had to infer vowel sounds from context. This worked for Phoenician (a Semitic language) but was problematic for Greek (an Indo-European language with a different linguistic structure). Greeks took several Phoenician consonant symbols that represented sounds Greek didn't use and converted them to vowels: alpha, epsilon, iota, omicron, and upsilon.

This adaptation created what we might call the first fully phonetic alphabet, a writing system in which symbols explicitly represent both consonant and vowel sounds. Anyone who learned this alphabet could, in theory, write anything in their language phonetically. This was more accessible and versatile than earlier writing systems. You didn't need years of scribal training to become literate. The Greek alphabet could be learned relatively quickly and used by anyone, not just professional scribes.

The alphabet spread rapidly across the Greek world, though different regions developed variant forms. Eventually, the Ionian version (used in Athens and much of eastern Greece) became standard. The Greek alphabet would later be adapted by the Romans into the Latin alphabet, which is still used across the Western world today. Greek letters are still used in mathematics and science (alpha, beta, gamma, delta, and so on).

Why did literacy matter so much? Written records allowed for new forms of social organization. Laws could be written down and publicly displayed, limiting interpretation by powerful judges. Contracts and commercial agreements could be recorded, helping trade. Government decisions could be documented, creating accountability and transparency.

Writing enabled new forms of cultural expression. Epic poetry could be recorded, preserving works like the *Iliad* and *Odyssey* that might otherwise have been lost or significantly altered over time. Lyric poetry flourished as poets like Sappho and Archilochus composed personal, emotional verses. Historical events could be documented, eventually leading to the birth of history as a discipline with Herodotus and Thucydides.

Philosophy emerged in the 6th and 5th centuries BCE partly because writing allowed complex arguments to be preserved and analyzed. Pre-Socratic philosophers like Thales, Anaximander, and Heraclitus could write down their theories about the nature of reality, allowing others to read, debate, and refine these ideas. Without writing, philosophy as a systematic discipline would have been far more difficult.

Political thought benefited from literacy. Written constitutions and law codes like those attributed to Lycurgus in Sparta or Solon in Athens established legal frameworks that could be referenced and debated. Political proposals could be drafted, circulated, and polished before being presented to assemblies. The later development of democracy in Athens would have been far more difficult without literacy to support its increasingly complex administration.

Science and mathematics advanced with written records. Observations could be documented and compared across time. Mathematical concepts could be worked out in writing and preserved for future study. The geometric proofs developed by later Greek mathematicians depended entirely on written notation.

Literacy was necessary for these developments, but it was not the sole cause. Political, economic, and cultural factors all contributed to the intellectual flowering of Classical Greece.

The rise of literacy also changed education. In oral cultures, education meant memorization and performance under the guidance of elders who held traditional knowledge. With writing, education could include reading texts, studying written works, and engaging with ideas from elsewhere. Libraries could preserve accumulated knowledge. Schools could use written texts to teach standardized curricula.

Not everyone became literate, of course. Literacy rates in ancient Greece are estimated by some scholars at perhaps 10 to 15 percent of the population at most, though precise figures are difficult to determine and likely varied considerably by time and place. Literacy was concentrated primarily among urban elites—the aristocrats, merchants, and scribes—while rural populations remained largely oral in their culture. Most Greeks remained illiterate throughout antiquity. However, even limited literacy transformed society. Literate individuals could read public inscriptions of laws and decrees. Professional scribes could write letters and contracts for illiterate clients. Written texts could be read aloud, making their content accessible to non-readers.

The Greeks recognized writing's importance. They attributed the alphabet's invention to the legendary Phoenician prince Cadmus, acknowledging their debt to Phoenician traders. They understood that writing was a tool that humans created and adapted for their own purposes. This awareness of writing as technology rather than a divine gift reflects the rational, pragmatic approach that would characterize much of Greek thought.

The adoption of the alphabet was one of those technological changes that enabled everything else. Without writing, there would have been no written law codes to limit aristocratic power, no preserved philosophy, no recorded history, no dramatic texts, and no geometry textbooks. Much of what we consider "classical Greek civilization" depended on literacy.

Chapter 4 – The Two Pillars: Athens and Sparta

The Iron Discipline: Spartan Life and Military System

If you had to pick two Greek city-states that represented opposite approaches to nearly everything, you'd pick Athens and Sparta. Athens would become famous for democracy, philosophy, art, and debate. Sparta became famous for one thing: war. Spartan society was dominated by military concerns to an extraordinary degree. Training, discipline, and combat readiness shaped nearly every aspect of citizen life. However, the Spartans weren't machines. They had religious festivals, social customs, and family bonds. Still, no Greek city came close to Sparta's single-minded focus on military excellence.

Sparta was located in the southern Peloponnese in a fertile valley called Lacedaemon (which is why Spartans were sometimes called Lacedaemonians). The city itself had no walls. This wasn't an oversight. Spartans believed their army was their wall. And they were right.

To understand Sparta, you need to understand how it came to be this way. Around 700 BCE, Spartans faced a problem: they needed more land. Their solution was to conquer their neighbors. They invaded Messenia, the region to their west, and after a brutal war, which lasted decades, they succeeded. However, instead of just taking the land and moving on, Spartans turned the conquered Messenians into helots–state-owned agricultural slaves bound to the land.

This created a new problem. Ancient sources claimed the helots outnumbered Spartans by at least seven to one, possibly more, though this figure might reflect Spartan fears more than an actual census; modern scholars debate the true ratio. What's certain is that helots vastly outnumbered Spartan citizens. The Spartans were sitting on top of a massive enslaved population that, understandably, hated them. The helots revolted in the 7th century BCE, and it took Sparta decades to crush the rebellion. This experience transformed Spartan society.

The Spartans realized that to maintain control over the helots, every Spartan male had to be a soldier, ready to suppress revolts at any moment. They couldn't afford weakness, and they couldn't afford distractions. They also couldn't afford to let citizens pursue their own interests. Sparta became a military society dedicated entirely to one purpose: staying strong enough to keep the helots enslaved.

Spartan boys were taken from their families at age seven and entered the *agoge*, the brutal state education and training system. From seven to eighteen, boys lived in barracks, trained constantly, and endured hardships designed to toughen them. According to various sources, they were deliberately underfed so they'd learn to steal food without getting caught. Getting caught meant punishment, not for stealing but for being clumsy enough to get caught. They slept on thin reed mats. They trained in combat, athletics, and endurance. They learned to endure pain without complaint.

Many stories about the agoge come from later sources, so they might be exaggerated or legendary, but the core truth is real. Spartan education was harsh. One famous story tells of a Spartan boy who stole a fox and hid it under his cloak. When questioned by his instructors, the fox began biting and clawing at the boy's stomach. The boy said nothing. He didn't move, letting the fox tear into him rather than admit he'd been caught. According to the story, he died from his wounds without making a sound. Whether this actually happened is questionable, but that Spartans told this story and admired the boy's behavior tells us what they valued.

At age twenty, if a young man passed his final tests, he became a full Spartan citizen-soldier. In theory, he remained a soldier ready for duty until age sixty. However, he still didn't live at home. Spartan men lived communally, eating together in mess groups called *syssitia*. Every night, Spartan citizens gathered with their mess groups to eat the same simple food, most famously a black broth made from boiled pork, vinegar, and salt that other Greeks found disgusting. One foreign visitor supposedly tasted it and said, "Now I understand why Spartans don't fear death."

Marriage existed in Sparta, but it was unlike marriage elsewhere in Greece. A Spartan man could marry, but he continued living in the barracks until age thirty. He would visit his wife secretly at night and return to the barracks before dawn. Only at thirty could a Spartan man finally live in his own household, though he still spent most of his time with his military unit and ate dinner with his mess group.

Why this extreme system? Because the Spartans believed that personal comfort and family ties made men soft. They wanted soldiers who were loyal to Sparta first, to their unit second, and to their family a distant third. They wanted men who would never break in battle because they had been trained since childhood to endure anything.

And it worked. Spartan hoplites were the finest infantry in Greece. In the phalanx formation, where discipline and cohesion mattered more than individual heroics, Spartans were unmatched. They drilled constantly, practicing maneuvers that other Greek armies attempted rarely, if at all. In battle, Spartan phalanxes didn't break. They didn't panic or run. Other Greeks feared facing Spartans on the battlefield because Spartans very rarely lost—at least, that was their fearsome reputation during the Archaic and early Classical periods.

Later sources describe Spartans fighting in perfect silence except for the sound of flutes keeping rhythm for their march. While other Greek armies charged into battle shouting and yelling, Spartans supposedly advanced slowly and steadily in complete formation, their long spears leveled, their shields locked, flutes playing. Whether this specific practice is historical or a literary trope that grew over time, the image captures how other Greeks saw Spartans: disciplined, professional, and terrifying.

Spartan society didn't just control men. It controlled women too, though in unexpected ways. Spartan women had more freedom and rights than women in most other Greek cities, though the extent of their independence is debated among historians and likely varied over time. They couldn't vote or hold office, but they could own property, manage estates, and speak more openly than their Athenian counterparts.

Why? Because Spartan men were always away training or fighting. Someone had to manage the estates, supervise the helots who worked the land, and handle business. That someone was Spartan women. They received physical education. This wasn't military training but rather athletics to make them strong and healthy for childbearing. Women were expected to produce strong sons for Sparta's army.

They were educated as well. Spartan women had a reputation for being outspoken and sharp-tongued. Plutarch recorded several sayings attributed to Spartan mothers. One, handing her son his shield as he left for war, supposedly told him, "Come back with this, or on it." In other words, she wanted him to return victorious or die in battle and be carried home on his shield. Don't come back defeated. This might be a legend, but it captures how Spartans thought about military honor.

The helots made this entire system possible. They worked the land, produced the food, and allowed Spartan citizens to spend all their time training. Without helots, Sparta couldn't function. But the helots were also Sparta's greatest vulnerability. If the helots ever successfully revolted, Spartan power would collapse.

Spartans dealt with this danger through various means of social control. According to some ancient sources, the Spartan state formally declared war on the helots each year. This wasn't an actual war; it was a legal fiction that allegedly allowed young Spartans in an elite unit called the *Krypteia* to hunt and kill any helot they deemed dangerous without legal consequences. Ancient sources describe the Krypteia going into the countryside at night to murder helots, particularly strong or intelligent ones who might lead a revolt. However, our sources on the Krypteia are fragmentary and contradictory, and modern historians debate the extent and nature of this institution. What's clear is that Sparta used terror and violence as tools to keep the helot population subjugated.

Sparta also had another class called *perioikoi*—"those who live around." These were free people living in towns around Sparta who weren't full Spartan citizens. They couldn't participate in Spartan political life, but they weren't enslaved. They worked as craftsmen, traders, and merchants, which were occupations that Spartan citizens considered beneath them. Perioikoi also fought in Sparta's army, though not in the elite front ranks, which were reserved for full citizens.

The Spartan government was complex and unusual. They kept two kings from two different royal families, and both ruled simultaneously. These kings led the army in war but had limited power at home. The real political power rested with five ephors—magistrates elected annually by the citizen assembly. The ephors could prosecute kings, conduct foreign policy, and run daily affairs. There was also the Gerousia, a council of twenty-eight elders over the age of sixty plus the two kings. The Gerousia proposed laws and served as a supreme court.

Spartans believed their system had been established by a legendary lawgiver named Lycurgus. According to tradition, Lycurgus went to the Oracle of Delphi, where he received divine approval for his laws. He made the Spartans swear they wouldn't change anything until he returned. Then he went into exile and never came back, binding Spartans to his system forever. This story is probably fiction, but Spartans believed it, which meant they considered their system divinely ordained and unchangeable.

This resistance to change became Sparta's fatal flaw. The system worked brilliantly for producing soldiers, but it was rigid and couldn't adapt. The Spartan population slowly declined, probably because so many died in warfare and because Spartan citizenship requirements were strict. By the Classical period, there were only a few thousand full Spartan citizens, though they ruled tens of thousands of helots and perioikoi.

However, in the Archaic and early Classical periods, Sparta was the dominant military power in Greece. Other city-states feared and respected the Spartans. When the Persian Empire threatened Greece, everyone looked to Sparta to lead the defense. Spartan soldiers at Thermopylae would become legendary. Spartan warriors at Plataea would help save Greece.

The price of this power was enormous. Spartans gave up art, philosophy, commerce, literature, and individual ambition. They lived under constant discipline, in fear of helot revolt, maintaining a system that required every generation to be as tough as the last. They created a society that was stable, powerful, and utterly foreign to how most Greeks lived.

Athens, as we're about to see, chose a different path entirely.

The Long Road to Self-Rule: Early Athenian Reform

While Sparta was building its military machine, Athens was stumbling toward something unprecedented: a political system where common citizens had real power. But Athens didn't start with democracy. It started with kings, moved to aristocratic oligarchy, experienced tyranny, and only then—through a series of reforms driven by crisis—eventually created democracy.

Athens occupied Attica, a large triangular peninsula in central Greece. Unlike many Greek regions, Attica had been unified under Athenian control early on, giving Athens a larger territory and population than most poleis. This would matter later, as more citizens meant more soldiers, more farmers, and eventually, more political participants.

According to tradition, Athens once had kings, but by the 7th century BCE, power had passed to aristocratic families who ruled through magistrates called archons. Nine archons were elected annually from aristocratic families. After serving, they joined the Areopagus, a council of ex-archons that held significant power. This was an oligarchy, or rule by wealthy landowners who made the laws, judged legal cases, and controlled policy.

For ordinary Athenians (small farmers, craftsmen, and traders), this system was increasingly oppressive. Land ownership was concentrated in fewer hands as wealthy families accumulated property. Poor farmers fell into debt, and Athenian law allowed creditors to enslave debtors who couldn't pay. Families lost their land and their freedom. Social tensions built toward a breaking point.

The first major reformer was Draco around 621 BCE. We know almost nothing about Draco himself, but we know he did something important. He wrote down Athens's laws and displayed them publicly. Before Draco, laws were unwritten and interpreted by aristocratic judges who could twist them however they wished. Even though most Athenians couldn't read them, written laws meant the laws themselves were fixed and couldn't be changed at a judge's whim. This limited manipulation of the justice system.

However, Draco's laws were notoriously harsh. The penalties for almost every offense, from murder to stealing a cabbage, were the same: death. Later Greeks joked that Draco's laws were written in blood, not ink. The word "draconian" still means an excessively severe law, derived from Draco's name. His harsh penalties didn't solve Athens's problems, as debt, land inequality, and social conflict remained.

By 594 BCE, Athens was on the verge of civil war. Rich and poor were ready to fight. The aristocrats needed someone both sides could trust to reform the system before violence erupted. They turned to Solon, an aristocrat who was also a respected poet and wise man. Both sides agreed to give Solon extraordinary powers to reform Athens's laws and constitution. What he did was remarkable.

A bust of Solon.[10]

Solon's first act was to cancel all debts secured by one's freedom. Athenian citizens who had been enslaved for debt were freed. Those who had been sold abroad as slaves were brought back at public expense. The practice of enslaving citizens for debt was abolished. This was the *seisachtheia*–the "shaking off of burdens." For ordinary Athenians drowning in debt, this was liberation.

But Solon didn't redistribute land, which disappointed the poor who wanted the aristocratic estates divided up. Solon believed in moderate reform, not revolution. He wanted to ease tensions without destroying the property rights that gave society stability. The rich weren't thrilled either. They'd lost some of their slaves and couldn't enslave debtors anymore. Solon later wrote that he'd given the people "as much power as they needed, nothing more," and that both rich and poor were unhappy with him, which meant he'd probably found the right balance.

Solon reorganized Athenian society into four classes based on wealth measured in agricultural production. The highest class, the *pentakosiomedimnoi* (those producing five hundred measures of grain or equivalent), could hold the highest offices, including archon. The second class, *hippeis* (cavalry, which referred to men who were wealthy enough to maintain a horse), could hold most offices. The third class, *zeugitai* (those who could afford hoplite armor), could hold minor offices. The fourth class, the *thetes* (wage laborers and the poor), couldn't hold office but could participate in the Assembly and law courts.

This system was still based on wealth, not birth. An aristocrat who lost his fortune dropped in class. A successful merchant or farmer who became wealthy could rise. It wasn't a democracy since the poor still couldn't hold office, but it was more open than a pure oligarchy based on noble bloodlines.

Solon also reformed Athens's government structure. He created a new council, the Boule of 400, with one hundred members from each of Athens's four traditional tribes. This council prepared business for the Assembly. He empowered the Assembly of all citizens to vote on laws and major decisions, though the aristocratic Areopagus still held significant power. He reformed the courts, allowing any citizen to bring prosecutions, not just victims or their families. This meant citizens could hold officials accountable.

Solon wrote new laws to replace most of Draco's harsh code, though he kept Draco's homicide laws. He encouraged trade and craft production, inviting foreign craftsmen to settle in Athens and even granting citizenship to whole families who moved to Athens to practice trades. He standardized weights and measures and promoted olive cultivation; Athens would become famous for exporting olive oil.

After completing his reforms, Solon left Athens for ten years. He'd made the Athenians swear they wouldn't change his laws while he was gone. This was shrewd since it forced the Athenians to live with the new system long enough to see if it worked rather than immediately undoing what they disliked.

Solon's reforms didn't solve everything. Tensions between the rich and poor remained. Different aristocratic factions competed for power. However, Solon had accomplished something important: he'd shown that reform was possible, that Athens's system could change without bloody civil war, and that ordinary citizens could have some voice in their own governance.

After Solon, Athens experienced a period of instability. Factions led by different aristocrats struggled for dominance. Eventually, around 561 BCE, one aristocrat named Pisistratus seized power and made himself tyrant. Remember, "tyrant" didn't necessarily mean brutal dictator; it meant someone who took power unconstitutionally. Pisistratus was actually quite popular.

Pisistratus promoted himself as a champion of the common people against the aristocracy. He was overthrown twice and came back twice, finally securing power around 546 BCE and ruling until his death in 527 BCE. During his rule, he redistributed some land from his aristocratic enemies to landless citizens. He provided loans to small farmers and promoted religious festivals, particularly the Panathenaea and the City Dionysia, which became major Athenian celebrations. Pisistratus commissioned building projects that employed workers and beautified Athens. He supported arts and culture; it's possible that the first written versions of Homer's epics were produced under his patronage.

Pisistratus didn't dismantle Solon's constitution, but he made sure his supporters held the offices. The Assembly still met, and the courts still functioned. However, real power rested with Pisistratus and his armed supporters. For ordinary Athenians, this was probably fine. Pisistratus was competent, relatively benign, and his policies benefited them.

Pisistratus's sons succeeded him. The older son, Hippias, ruled capably at first, but the younger son, Hipparchus, was murdered in 514 BCE by two men, Harmodius and Aristogeiton, in a personal vendetta over a love affair. Athenians later mythologized Harmodius and Aristogeiton as tyrannicides, though. They were seen as heroes who struck a blow for freedom. Statues of them were erected in the agora, and they became symbols of resistance to tyranny.

After Hipparchus's death, Hippias became paranoid and oppressive. His rule grew harsh. Aristocratic families schemed against him. One faction, the Alcmaeonids, was in exile and wanted back into Athens. They enlisted help from Sparta, which opposed tyranny, even though Sparta itself was hardly free. In 510 BCE, a Spartan army invaded Attica, besieged the tyrants on the Acropolis, and forced Hippias into exile.

The Peisistratid tyranny was over. Athens was free from tyranny. But what would replace it? Different aristocratic factions competed to dominate the new government. One faction, led by Isagoras, represented the traditional aristocracy. The other, led by Cleisthenes of the Alcmaeonid family, took a different approach. Cleisthenes positioned himself as a reformer and won the support of the common people by proposing radical changes that would give them real political power.

What Cleisthenes did next would transform Athens forever.

Inventing Democracy: Cleisthenes and the Citizen Body

In 508 BCE, Cleisthenes did something revolutionary. Facing opposition from aristocratic rivals, he took his case to the *demos*–the common people–and promised them a share of political power if they supported him. They did, and Cleisthenes delivered. What he created wasn't just a reform of the Athenian government. It was a fundamentally new system: *demokratia*, rule by the demos.

The word "democracy" literally means "power of the people." However, what Cleisthenes created was more specific. It was a direct democracy in which citizens participated personally in making laws and decisions, not a representative democracy in which citizens elect others to govern for them. Every male citizen had the right–and the responsibility–to participate directly in governing Athens.

Cleisthenes's reforms were brilliant in their design. His goal was to break the power of traditional aristocratic families and redistribute political influence more broadly. He did this by completely reorganizing how Athens was structured.

Previously, Athens was divided into four traditional tribes based on kinship ties and controlled by aristocratic families. Cleisthenes reorganized the political role of these tribes and created ten new tribes by artificial means. Each new tribe was made up of *demes* (local districts or villages) from three different regions of Attica: the city, the coast, and the inland. These demes were distributed so that each tribe contained a mix of citizens from different regions and different social backgrounds.

This was genius. The new tribes had no historical basis and no traditional aristocratic leadership. Citizens' primary political identity shifted from their family to their tribe and deme. Aristocrats still existed and still had influence, but they could no longer automatically control blocs of voters based on kinship networks. Political competition opened up as a result.

Each tribe contributed fifty men to a new council, the Boule of 500 (which replaced Solon's Boule of 400). The Boule prepared business for the Assembly, managed daily administration, oversaw finances, and handled foreign relations. Members were selected by lot from citizens over thirty, and they served one-year terms. Any citizen could serve, though no one could serve more than twice in a lifetime. Selection by lottery meant every citizen had an equal chance of serving. This rotated political experience throughout the citizen body rather than concentrating it in a small elite.

The Assembly—the Ekklesia—became the supreme governing body of Athens. Any male citizen over eighteen could attend, speak, and vote. The Assembly met on the Pnyx, a hill west of the Acropolis, about forty times a year. Thousands of citizens would gather to debate laws, declare war, approve treaties, vote on taxes, decide whether to ostracize someone, and handle virtually every major decision Athens made.

This was direct democracy in action. When Athens decided to go to war, the decision was made by citizens who would do the fighting. When Athens passed a law, the citizens who would live under that law voted on it. When Athens approved a budget, citizens who would pay taxes or benefit from public spending made the choice.

The courts also became more democratic. Large juries of citizens, sometimes hundreds of people, heard cases. Jurors were selected by lot from volunteers. Both the prosecution and defense were presented by the parties themselves, not by professional lawyers. The jury voted by secret ballot, and the majority ruled. This meant that legal cases were decided by masses of ordinary citizens, not by aristocratic judges.

Cleisthenes introduced one more innovation: ostracism. Once a year, the Assembly could vote to exile any citizen for ten years without trial and without confiscating his property. Citizens wrote a name on a broken piece of pottery—an *ostrakon*—and the person with the most votes (if at least six thousand votes were cast) was exiled. This was meant as a safety valve to remove potential tyrants or politicians who were becoming too powerful, preventing civil war by peacefully removing troublemakers.

Did Cleisthenes's system constitute democracy as we'd recognize it? Yes and no. It was democracy for those who counted as citizens, but that was a minority of Athens's population. Women couldn't participate.

Slaves couldn't participate. Metics (foreign residents) couldn't participate, even if they'd lived in Athens for generations. Only free adult males born to Athenian citizen parents could participate.

Even among citizens, participation wasn't equal. Wealthy citizens had more time to engage in politics because they didn't need to work constantly to survive. They could speak more persuasively because they were better educated. In practice, aristocrats and wealthy citizens still dominated Athenian politics, but they dominated through persuasion and election, not by birthright. Any citizen could challenge them, propose laws, or speak in the Assembly.

The system also had problems. Direct democracy can be chaotic. Popular speakers could sway the Assembly with emotional appeals. The poor majority could vote to seize wealth from the rich. Decisions made in the heat of the moment could prove disastrous. Athens would eventually make some terrible choices through democratic vote, which we'll see during the Peloponnesian War.

But the system also had strengths. It gave ordinary citizens real investment in their polis. Citizens served in government, fought in the military, and participated in courts. They weren't passive subjects; they were active participants. This created loyalty and engagement that Athens's enemies couldn't match. When Athenians fought to defend their city, they were literally defending their own government, laws, and decisions.

The system also rotated political experience. Because offices were filled by lot and because jury service was open to all, thousands of citizens gained practical experience in governance. This wasn't professional politicians ruling over passive masses. This was citizens governing themselves, learning by doing.

The Boule of 500 is a good example. Each tribe's fifty representatives rotated in serving as the executive committee—the *prytaneis*—for one-tenth of the year. During their thirty-six days in charge, one member was selected by lot each day to serve as chairman. This meant that in a given year, five hundred different citizens held some governmental responsibility, and fifty served in top administrative positions. Over a generation, thousands of citizens would have direct experience running Athens.

Democracy developed further over the next decades. Pericles later introduced pay for jury service and attending Assembly meetings, which allowed poorer citizens to participate more fully. The system evolved and adapted. However, the core principle Cleisthenes established remained: citizens governing themselves through direct participation.

Athens's democracy was an experiment. No other major city had tried anything like it. Most Greek cities remained oligarchies or were ruled by tyrants. Sparta, the military powerhouse, had a mixed constitution that was definitely not democratic. Other Greeks looked at Athenian democracy with skepticism or horror. Giving power to the many seemed like a recipe for chaos. How could ignorant farmers and craftsmen make complex policy decisions? How could you prevent rabblerousers from manipulating the mob?

These were fair questions, and Athenian democracy would indeed struggle with these problems. But Athens also showed that democracy could work. The city would become wealthy, powerful, and culturally brilliant while governed by its citizens. Ordinary citizens would help defeat the Persian Empire. Athenian democracy would become Athens's proudest achievement and would inspire political thought for the next 2,500 years.

Cleisthenes didn't create democracy alone. He built on Solon's reforms and learned from tyranny's failures. He responded to the political crisis with creative solutions, and he succeeded because ordinary Athenians supported him and wanted political power. But Cleisthenes designed the system and deserves credit as democracy's founding figure, even if later Athenians sometimes forgot his name while celebrating their democratic achievements.

By 500 BCE, Athens had been transformed. It was now a democracy. Sparta remained a stable military oligarchy focused entirely on war. These two visions of the polis—democratic Athens and militaristic Sparta—would define Greek politics for the next century. They would soon need each other to survive the Persian invasion, and then they would spend decades fighting over which system should dominate Greece.

Cultural Crossroads: Comparing and Contrasting the Two

Athens and Sparta weren't just different; they were opposite in almost every way that mattered. If you dropped an Athenian in Sparta or a Spartan in Athens, they'd be utterly confused by how the other city lived. Let's compare them directly to understand just how different two Greek cities could be.

Government: Athens was a democracy where thousands of citizens participated directly in political decisions. The Assembly made laws. Juries decided court cases. Officials were selected by lot or elected for short terms. Every citizen could speak, vote, and serve. Sparta was an oligarchy with two kings, five ephors, a council of elders, and an assembly that mostly rubber-stamped decisions made by others. Political power rested with a small group of elites. The system was designed for stability, not participation.

Military: Sparta's entire society was organized around producing superior soldiers. Spartan male citizens were expected to serve as warriors from age twenty to sixty, training constantly and fighting in what was widely considered the finest phalanx in Greece. Athens relied on citizen-soldiers who were farmers and craftsmen most of the year and warriors when needed. Athenian hoplites were capable but not an elite fighting force like the Spartans. Athens's military strength came from numbers and especially from its navy, which became the largest in Greece.

Social Structure: Sparta had three classes: Spartan citizens (a small minority), perioikoi (free non-citizens), and helots (enslaved agricultural workers who vastly outnumbered citizens). The entire system depended on helot labor, which meant Spartans lived in constant fear of revolt. Athens had citizens, metics (foreign residents), and slaves. Slavery existed in Athens, but it wasn't as central to the economy. More Athenians worked their own land or practiced trades.

Women: Spartan women had more freedoms than women in most other Greek cities. They could own property, manage estates, and exercise. They were educated and could speak more openly than women elsewhere. They had to run things while men were away training or fighting. Athenian women were restricted to the household. They couldn't own property, participate in politics, or appear in public without a male guardian. Upper-class Athenian women lived secluded lives focused on managing households and raising children. Working-class women had more freedom by necessity, but they still had no political rights.

Economy: Sparta despised trade and commerce. Citizens couldn't engage in business, as it was considered beneath them. They lived off the produce of helot labor on their land. Sparta deliberately discouraged the accumulation of wealth and commercial activity, though exactly how they did this is debated; later sources mention iron bars, but archaeological evidence for such practices is lacking. Athens embraced commerce. It became the busiest port in Greece, trading olive oil, wine, pottery, and silver throughout the Mediterranean. Athenian merchants and craftsmen grew wealthy. The city's prosperity came from trade, not just agriculture.

Education: Spartan education was the agoge, a brutal military training system that started from age seven. It was focused on creating tough, obedient soldiers. Boys learned to fight, endure pain, and obey orders. That's about it. There was no philosophy, literature, or art in Spartan education. Athens valued intellectual development. Boys learned reading, writing, mathematics, music, poetry, and athletics. Wealthy families hired tutors. As Athens grew prosperous, philosophy, rhetoric, and debate became central to education. Athens produced philosophers, while Sparta produced soldiers.

Culture: Sparta produced far less art, architecture, literature, or philosophy than Athens, especially after the full institutionalization of its military system. Early Sparta, in the Archaic period, actually had significant cultural and artistic production, but as the military ethos hardened, this largely ceased. Classical Sparta wrote a few poems, mostly about war and duty. Their buildings were plain. They avoided luxury and beauty, seeing them as corrupting influences. Athens became the cultural capital of Greece. Athenians built the Parthenon and other magnificent temples. They developed drama, both tragedy and comedy. Philosophers like Socrates walked Athenian streets. Historians like Herodotus and Thucydides wrote there. Sculptors, painters, and poets flocked to Athens. Athens cared about beauty, wisdom, and art. Sparta didn't, at least not by the Classical period.

Values: Sparta valued obedience, discipline, endurance, military excellence, and stability. The ideal Spartan was tough, brave, loyal to the state, and willing to die without hesitation. Individual desires didn't matter. Spartans were supposed to be identical, interchangeable parts in a military machine. Athens valued freedom, creativity, ambition, wisdom, and achievement. The ideal Athenian was versatile. He would be good at speaking, thinking, fighting if necessary, and contributing to civic life. Individual excellence was celebrated. Athenians competed with each other constantly to prove their worth.

Foreign Policy: Sparta led the Peloponnesian League, a network of allied cities that followed Sparta's lead in military matters. Sparta generally left allies alone as long as they provided troops when asked. Sparta rarely went far from home and didn't seek to build an empire. Athens created an empire. It started as the leader of the Delian League, a defensive alliance against Persia, but Athens gradually turned allies into subjects, demanding tribute and interfering in their governments. Athens was aggressive, expansionist, and imperialistic.

Despite these differences, Athens and Sparta had important similarities. Both were Greek. Both spoke Greek (though different dialects). Both worshiped the same gods. Both competed in the Olympic Games. Both valued courage and honored military achievement. Both excluded women, slaves, and foreigners from citizenship. Both believed Greeks were superior to barbarians. Both loved their polis intensely and would fight to defend it.

But the differences mattered more. These two cities represented different answers to questions about how society should be organized, what values should matter most, and what humans should strive for. Sparta chose order, stability, and military excellence at the cost of freedom and culture. Athens chose freedom, creativity, and individual ambition at the cost of stability and order.

Here's the interesting thing: Greeks at the time recognized that both systems had merits. Some admired Sparta's relative stability (though it is important to note that Sparta did face population decline, economic pressures, and the constant threat of helot revolt), its discipline, and its military prowess. The Spartan system changed slowly compared to more volatile cities. Sparta had fewer tyrants and less frequent civil wars than many poleis. Spartans were the best soldiers in Greece. There was something appealing about that consistency and martial excellence.

Others preferred Athens's energy, creativity, and freedom. Athens was dynamic and innovative. It produced art and ideas that influenced all of Greece. Athenian democracy gave citizens a voice in their own governance. There was something appealing about that freedom and intellectual life.

Both cities would soon face their greatest test. When Persia invaded Greece in 492 BCE, Athens and Sparta would need to work together to survive. After the Persian threat ended, they would spend decades fighting each other to determine which system would dominate Greece. The rivalry between Athens and Sparta would shape Greek history throughout the Classical period.

For now, in the early 5th century BCE, both cities had reached their mature forms. Sparta was the dominant land power, its army feared throughout Greece. Athens was a rising democracy, its navy growing. The stage was set for the next great chapter in Greek history: the moment when Greeks would prove themselves against the superpower of their age. The Persians were coming, and everything was about to change.

Chapter 5 – Fire and Freedom: The Persian Wars

Trouble in the East: The Ionian Revolt

By 500 BCE, the Greek world extended far beyond mainland Greece. Greek cities dotted the coast of Asia Minor, the western edge of what is now Turkey. These were wealthy, cultured cities: Miletus, Ephesus, Phocaea, and dozens of others. Miletus was one of the richest cities in the Greek world. It was a center of philosophy and traded with colonies stretching from Egypt to the Black Sea. These cities had marble temples, bustling harbors, and populations that spoke Greek and worshiped Greek gods. The people considered themselves Greek, though after centuries of interaction with non-Greek peoples and the development of distinct local identities, Ionian Greek identity was more complex than simply equating them with mainland Greeks.

But they had a problem. They weren't free.

These cities, collectively called Ionia, had fallen under Persian control decades earlier when the Persian king Cyrus conquered the Lydian kingdom that had previously ruled them. The Persian Empire, which had conquered everything from Egypt to India, was the superpower of the ancient world. Compared to Persia, the Greek cities were tiny, insignificant specks on the edge of the empire. Persian kings barely noticed them; they were just another group of subjects paying tribute.

Persian rule wasn't necessarily brutal by ancient standards. The Persians generally allowed subject peoples to maintain their own customs, worship their own gods, and govern their own local affairs as long as taxes were paid and loyalty was maintained. But Persian rule still chafed. The Persians installed tyrants to govern the Ionian cities, ensuring loyalty to the Persian king. These tyrants were Greeks themselves, but they ruled for Persia's benefit, not their cities'. Taxes flowed to the Persian court at Susa. Persian satraps (provincial governors) interfered in local affairs when it suited them. Young Ionian men were conscripted to fight in Persian wars that weren't their concern.

Meanwhile, across the Aegean, Greeks in cities like Athens were experimenting with democracy and self-governance. The Ionians saw their mainland cousins enjoying freedom while they lived under foreign domination. The contrast grew more painful with each passing year.

In 499 BCE, the situation exploded. The tyrant of Miletus, a man named Aristagoras, had a problem. He had persuaded the Persians to let him lead an expedition to conquer the wealthy island of Naxos, promising it would be easy and profitable. It wasn't. The expedition failed miserably, and Aristagoras had spent Persian money with nothing to show for it. He feared the Persian king would punish him for the failure, possibly removing him from power or worse.

Facing potential removal or execution, Aristagoras made a desperate gamble. He gave up his tyranny, declared Miletus a democracy, and called on the other Ionian cities to revolt against Persian rule. It was a calculated move. Aristagoras needed allies and popular support if he was going to survive Persian retaliation, and positioning himself as a champion of freedom rather than a tyrant served his purposes.

It was also audacious. The Persian Empire had hundreds of thousands of soldiers, vast resources, and a reputation for crushing rebellions with overwhelming force. When the Babylonians had revolted a generation earlier, Darius had besieged their city for nearly two years and then impaled three thousand of their leaders. The Ionians knew what they were risking. Even united, they were no match for Persia militarily.

However, the appeal of freedom proved irresistible. City after city joined the revolt. Persian-appointed tyrants were overthrown or fled. Democratic governments were established in their place. For the first time in decades, the Ionian cities were governing themselves. It felt like liberation.

Aristagoras knew this wouldn't last without external help, which was why he crossed the Aegean to seek support from mainland Greece. He went to Sparta first. Sparta had the best army in Greece, and Aristagoras hoped Spartan soldiers might tip the balance. He met with King Cleomenes and tried to persuade him to help. According to Herodotus, Aristagoras brought a bronze map—possibly the first map Cleomenes had ever seen—showing how rich the Persian Empire was and how much gold and silver awaited any army that could defeat it. He pointed out all the peoples Persia had conquered, emphasizing how easily the Persians might be defeated by superior Greek warriors.

But Cleomenes asked a practical question: how far was it from the Ionian coast to the Persian capital at Susa? When Aristagoras admitted it was a three-month journey inland, Cleomenes refused. Sparta didn't campaign that far from home. The logistics were impossible, the risks were enormous, and Sparta had no interest in foreign adventures. Aristagoras was ordered to leave Sparta before sunset.

Aristagoras had better luck in Athens. Athens had historical ties to Ionia. Athenians considered the Ionians their kinsmen, fellow members of the Ionian ethnic group who had migrated to Asia Minor from Attica centuries earlier. Athens had recently established its democracy under Cleisthenes and perhaps felt sympathy for the Ionians trying to throw off tyranny. Or maybe Athens simply saw an opportunity to strike at Persia, gain influence in Asia Minor, and access the region's wealth. Whatever the reason, the Athenian Assembly voted to send twenty ships to support the revolt. The city of Eretria on the island of Euboea, which also had ties to Ionia, sent five more.

Twenty-five ships weren't much—maybe five thousand soldiers total—but they were enough to encourage the Ionians and raise hopes that mainland support might grow. The revolt spread from city to city. Persian-installed tyrants were overthrown, and democratic governments were established. For a moment, it looked like the Ionians might actually succeed.

In 498 BCE, the Ionian forces, reinforced by the Athenian and Eretrian ships, marched inland to Sardis, the capital of the Persian satrapy of Lydia and one of the richest cities in the empire. They caught the Persians by surprise and captured the lower city, though the citadel remained in Persian hands. A fire broke out, but whether it was intentional or accidental isn't clear. Herodotus suggests it started when a soldier set fire to a reed house, and the flames spread uncontrollably through the city. The fire at Sardis destroyed a temple sacred to the local goddess Cybele, an act that would later be used to justify Persian retaliation against Greek temples.

But the success was short-lived. A Persian counterattack caught the Greek forces retreating from Sardis and defeated them at the Battle of Ephesus. The Athenians and Eretrians, spooked by the defeat and perhaps realizing they'd bitten off more than they could chew, sailed home and refused to send further help. Herodotus notes dryly that these twenty ships were "the beginning of evils for both Greeks and barbarians." They had accomplished little militarily but had given Persia a reason to view mainland Greece as an enemy.

The Ionians were on their own. The revolt continued for five more years, but the outcome was never really in doubt. Persia had unlimited resources and manpower. The Persian king, Darius I, methodically reconquered the rebel cities one by one. Persian armies besieged towns, and the Persian fleets blockaded harbors. City walls were breached. Populations were massacred or enslaved. Refugees fled from city to city as the Persian noose tightened.

By 494 BCE, only Miletus held out. The Persians assembled a massive fleet—reportedly six hundred ships drawn from their Phoenician, Egyptian, and Cypriot subjects—and besieged Miletus by land and sea. The Ionians gathered their own ships for a final naval battle at Lade, an island near Miletus. They had about 350 ships; they were outnumbered, but not impossibly so. If they could win at sea, they could break the blockade and prolong the war.

But their unity crumbled. Some contingents, particularly the Samians, had been bribed or persuaded by Persia to defect. Others lost their nerve. During the battle, much of the Ionian fleet fled or switched sides. The Persians won decisively. With naval superiority secure, they besieged and captured Miletus. The city that had sparked the revolt was destroyed as an example. Most of its population was killed or enslaved. The male survivors were deported to the mouth of the Tigris River deep in the Persian Empire, separated from their homeland forever. Women and children were enslaved.

The destruction was so complete and the suffering so intense that when news reached Athens, a playwright named Phrynichus produced a tragedy called *The Capture of Miletus*. The Athenian audience wept openly in the theater and then fined Phrynichus for reminding them of their own failures and the fate of their kinsmen. The play was banned from ever being performed again.

The Ionian Revolt was over. The cities were punished harshly, though some ancient sources suggest Persia eventually granted certain cities more local autonomy than before, possibly even allowing democratic forms of government in some cases, though the extent of such reforms remains debated, and Persian oversight continued. The empire had learned from the revolt.

So had the Greeks. They'd learned that Persia could be hurt, that Persian armies could be beaten, and that unity among Greek cities was nearly impossible to maintain. They'd also learned that Persia didn't forget insults. King Darius hadn't forgotten that Athens and Eretria had helped burn Sardis. Darius reportedly had a servant remind him three times at every dinner, "Master, remember the Athenians."

The Ionian Revolt had been the opening move in a larger conflict that would determine whether Greeks would remain free or become subjects of the Persian king. The mainland Greeks had just painted a target on themselves, and they had no idea what was about to hit them.

The Shock of Marathon: First Invasion

In 492 BCE, Darius launched his first strike against mainland Greece. He sent an army under his son-in-law Mardonius across the Hellespont, the strait separating Asia from Europe, into Thrace, conquering territory along the northern Aegean coast. However, a storm destroyed much of the Persian fleet off Mount Athos, and the expedition was recalled. It was a setback, not a defeat. Darius was far from finished.

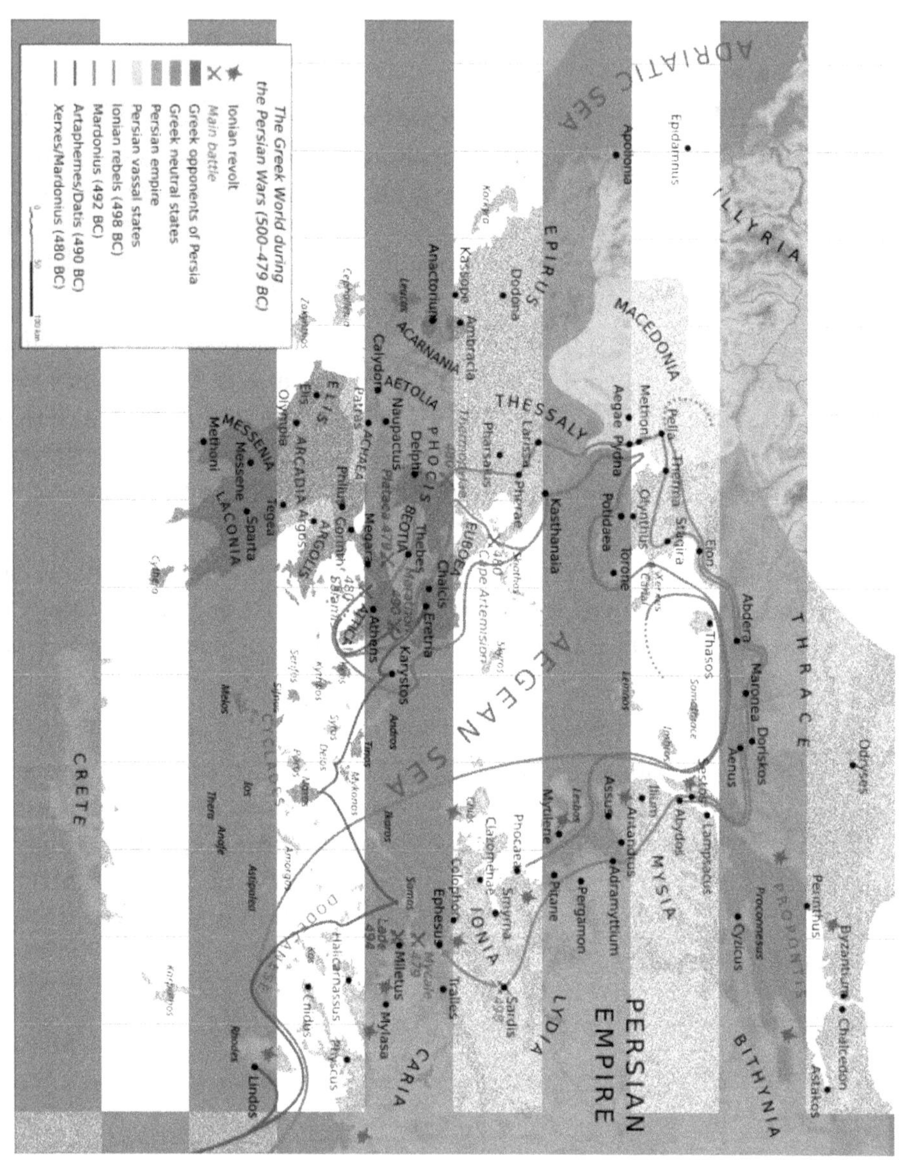

The Greek world during the Greco-Persian Wars.[11]

Two years later, in 490 BCE, Darius tried again with a different strategy. Instead of marching an army overland through difficult terrain, he sent a naval expedition directly across the Aegean. A fleet carrying perhaps twenty-five thousand soldiers–the numbers are disputed, but it was substantial–sailed from island to island, accepting the submission of Greek cities along the way. Most surrendered without fighting. Resistance seemed pointless.

The fleet's first major target was Eretria on Euboea, which had helped the Ionians burn Sardis. After a brief siege, the city fell through betrayal. The Persians enslaved the entire population and burned the city's temples in revenge for Sardis. Then the fleet crossed the narrow strait to mainland Greece and landed at Marathon, a coastal plain about twenty-six miles northeast of Athens.

Marathon was chosen deliberately. It offered a good beach for landing ships, open ground suitable for Persian cavalry, and was near enough to Athens to threaten the city directly. There was also a political dimension. The Persians brought Hippias, the old Athenian tyrant who had been expelled in 510 BCE, with them. The Persians intended to reinstall him as Athens's ruler, making Athens a Persian client state.

Athens faced a desperate situation. A Persian army sat less than a day's march from the city. Most Greek cities had already submitted to Persia. Sparta, the only power that could help, was celebrating a religious festival and claimed its laws forbade the army from marching until the moon was full. Athens was effectively alone.

The Athenians made a courageous decision. Instead of cowering behind the city walls and hoping the Persians would go away, they marched out to meet them. The Athenian army–about ten thousand hoplites plus perhaps one thousand men from the small city of Plataea, which honored its alliance with Athens even when larger cities stayed home–took a position in the hills overlooking the Marathon plain, blocking the roads to Athens.

It was an aggressive move born of necessity. The Athenians couldn't simply wait in Athens for a siege. They didn't have enough food stored for a prolonged blockade, and the Persian fleet could land troops anywhere along the coast. It was better to engage the enemy on the ground of their choosing, where the hills protected their flanks and prevented the Persian cavalry from maneuvering around them.

For several days, the two armies faced each other without fighting. The Athenian generals debated what to do. Athens had ten generals at this time, each commanding in rotation. Some argued they should wait for Spartan reinforcements since Sparta had promised to send its army after the religious festival ended. Others, including a general named Miltiades, who had lived under Persian rule and understood how the Persians fought, argued they should attack immediately. The longer they waited, he argued, the more likely Persian cavalry would overwhelm them, or the

Persians would load their troops back on ships and sail directly to an undefended Athens.

Miltiades had another worry. He knew that some Athenians were in contact with the Persians. These sympathizers might betray the city if they thought a Persian victory was inevitable. The longer this standoff continued, the more likely treachery became. Athens needed a decisive victory, and they needed it soon.

The deadlock broke when scouts reported that the Persian cavalry had been sent away from the camp—or so the Greeks believed. The question of where the Persian cavalry was during the battle remains one of history's great debates. Ancient sources suggest they might have been loading back onto ships, possibly preparing to sail around to Athens while the main Persian force kept the Greek army pinned at Marathon, but this is an interpretation rather than a known fact. What's clear is that the Persians fought without cavalry support. This was Athens's moment. Without cavalry to protect their flanks and threaten the Greek formation, the Persian infantry was vulnerable.

Miltiades convinced the other generals to attack. It was his day to command, and he made his move. The Athenian hoplites formed their phalanx, eight ranks deep in the center but possibly deeper on the wings, and began advancing across the plain toward the Persian position about a mile away.

As they drew closer, perhaps when they came within range of Persian arrows, the order was given to charge. The Athenians broke into a run. This was not a mindless sprint that would exhaust them, but a steady jog in formation that covered ground quickly while keeping the phalanx together. This was unprecedented. Greeks didn't charge at a run. However, Miltiades understood that every second his men spent under Persian fire would weaken them before they even reached the enemy line.

The Persians were accustomed to enemies who fled from their arrows or were pinned down by archery before the hand-to-hand fighting even started, so they were astonished to see Greeks charging directly at them in formation. Herodotus says the Persians thought the Athenians were insane "since they were few and yet were charging at a run, having neither cavalry nor archers." The Persians were about to learn that discipline and heavy armor could defeat arrows if the enemy closed the distance fast enough.

The battle that followed was vicious and chaotic. The Persian center, composed of their best troops, pushed back the Athenian center and threatened to break through. The Athenian line bent inward as the Persian center advanced. This was dangerous. If the Persian center broke through completely, they could split the Greek army and attack it from behind.

But the Athenian wings, reinforced by Miltiades's strategic decision to strengthen the flanks at the center's expense, defeated the forces opposite them, which included Greek mercenaries and subject peoples who weren't as motivated or well trained as the Persian core troops. Then, in a move that required remarkable discipline and communication, the Athenian wings didn't pursue their defeated enemies. Instead, they wheeled inward and attacked the Persian center from both sides.

The Persian army, which moments before had been on the verge of victory, suddenly found itself enveloped, being hit from three directions at once. The Persian troops in the center, which were already engaged with the Athenian center to their front, now had Athenian hoplites crashing into their flanks. The formation broke. What had been a disciplined army became a mob of men trying to survive.

The Persian army shattered and ran for their ships beached on the shore. The Athenians pursued, fighting all the way to the water's edge. This was the most dangerous moment for the Persians. The soldiers were weighed down with equipment, exhausted from fighting, and trying to wade through surf and scramble onto ships while Greek hoplites stabbed and hacked at them from behind. Men drowned in their armor. Ships pushed off from shore with soldiers desperately clinging to the sides.

The fighting in the surf was particularly fierce when the Athenians tried to capture the beached ships. They succeeded in taking seven vessels, but it cost lives. One Athenian, Cynegeirus, supposedly grabbed the stern of a Persian ship and had his hand cut off by an axe. His brother, the playwright Aeschylus, who would later write tragedies performed throughout Greece, also fought at Marathon. He was prouder of this service than of any of his theatrical achievements.

According to Herodotus, the Persians lost about 6,400 men killed. The Athenians lost 192, though modern historians suspect this suspiciously specific figure might be a commemorative number rather than an actual casualty count. It possibly represents the number of men buried in the burial mound. Whatever the precise numbers, there's no doubt the Athenian victory was decisive. The Persian army, which had seemed unstoppable, had been beaten in open battle by a smaller Greek force.

Among the Athenian dead was the polemarch Callimachus, who had cast the deciding vote in favor of Miltiades's plan to attack. His body was later recovered and buried with honors. Also killed was Stesilaus, one of the ten generals. But the victory belonged to Miltiades, who had understood Persian tactics, recognized the moment to attack, and led the Athenians to an astonishing triumph.

However, the battle wasn't quite over. The Persian fleet didn't sail away in defeat. It sailed south, rounding Cape Sounion and heading for Athens itself. The city was virtually undefended. If the Persians could land their army at Athens before the Greek soldiers returned from Marathon, they could capture the city unopposed. Some Persians might have hoped that Athenian traitors would open the gates for them.

The Athenian army force-marched back to Athens. According to tradition, they covered the twenty-six miles in full armor—probably fifty to sixty pounds of equipment—in time to man the city's defenses before the Persian fleet arrived. This was an extraordinary feat of endurance. The soldiers had just fought a brutal battle, pursued fleeing enemies for miles, and now had to march home at speed while wearing heavy armor under the hot Greek sun.

When the Persian fleet rounded the point and saw the Athenian army standing ready on the shore, drawn up in battle formation, the Persian commanders decided they'd had enough. They turned their ships around and sailed back to Asia. There would be no victory for Persia this year. The expedition that was supposed to punish Athens for helping the Ionian rebels ended in defeat and humiliation.

The Battle of Marathon became instantly legendary. It was celebrated as the moment Greeks proved their courage, and it showed that a love of freedom could overcome the vast might of a despotic empire. The 192 Athenians who died were buried on the battlefield under a great mound, the Soros, that still stands today. They were honored as heroes who saved not just Athens but also the Greek way of life itself.

One legend connected to Marathon, though it was not recorded until centuries later and is probably not historical, tells of a messenger named Pheidippides. According to the story, he first ran from Athens to Sparta—roughly 140 miles—in just two days before the battle to request Spartan aid. Then, after the Athenian victory, he ran from Marathon to Athens to announce the triumph, shouting "Nenikēkamen!" ("We have won!") before collapsing dead from exhaustion. This story, whether true or not, inspired the modern marathon race of 26.2 miles, commemorating the legendary run from the battlefield to Athens and an ancient Greek victory that changed history.

The Battle of Marathon also had profound political consequences. It elevated Athens's status among Greek cities. Before Marathon, Athens was important but not dominant. After Marathon, Athens had defeated the Persian Empire virtually alone, with help only from tiny Plataea. This gave the Athenians immense confidence in their democracy, army, and destiny. It showed that free citizens fighting for their own city could match or exceed professional soldiers fighting for an empire. The victory validated the democratic experiment and convinced the Athenians they were special.

For Miltiades, the hero of Marathon, the aftermath was bittersweet. He led an expedition to attack Persian-controlled islands the following year, but it failed, and he was wounded. The Athenians, ungrateful or simply realistic about military failure, prosecuted him for the expedition's costs. He died of his infected wound before the trial ended. Athens honored heroes but didn't tolerate failure, even from those who had saved the city.

Marathon didn't end the Persian threat. If anything, it made it worse. Darius began preparing a much larger expedition to crush Greece once and for all. He died in 486 BCE before he could launch it, but his son Xerxes inherited both the Persian throne and his father's determination to punish Greece. The Persians would return, and next time, they would bring an army so large that all of Greece combined might not be able to stop it.

The Lion at the Gate: Thermopylae

For ten years after Marathon, Greece waited for the Persian revenge that everyone knew was coming. The delay wasn't because Persia had given up; it was because Darius died in 486 BCE, and his son Xerxes first had to secure his throne, then suppress a major revolt in Egypt, and then deal with unrest in Babylon before turning his attention back to Greece. However, Xerxes never forgot his father's obsession with punishing the Greeks.

When Xerxes finally moved in 480 BCE, he did so on an unprecedented scale. This wouldn't be a raid or a punitive expedition. This would be a full-scale invasion intended to conquer Greece entirely and incorporate it permanently into the Persian Empire. Ancient sources claim his army numbered over one million men. Herodotus famously described the army drinking rivers dry as it passed. Modern historians estimate the actual force was probably between 100,000 and 300,000 soldiers, which is still enormous by ancient standards and larger than any army Greece could hope to field.

The Persians spent years preparing for this invasion. They stockpiled supplies at depots along the invasion route. They dug a canal through the Athos peninsula, which is over a mile long, to avoid the storms that had wrecked the previous Persian fleet there. They constructed two boat bridges across the Hellespont by lashing hundreds of ships together side by side. When storms destroyed the first bridges, Xerxes allegedly had the engineers executed and ordered the sea itself whipped three hundred times as punishment, which tells you something about how the Persians viewed obstacles.

The army that crossed into Europe was truly multinational. The Persian Empire's strength came from conscripting soldiers from all its subject peoples. There were Persians and Medes in their elaborate armor, Babylonians and Assyrians with their bronze helmets and linen breastplates, Egyptians with their wooden shields and curved swords, Indians with cotton clothing and bamboo bows, Ethiopians wearing leopard and lion skins, and Thracians with fox-skin caps. There were Phrygians, Armenians, Lydians, Carians, and Ionians–dozens of peoples, each with their own equipment, marching under Persian command. The army must have been an incredible sight.

Xerxes brought his household, court, harem, and throne. He brought everything needed to rule an empire. It is possible that he planned to stay in Greece and govern it personally once it was conquered. The fleet that accompanied the army numbered perhaps six hundred to eight hundred warships plus hundreds of transport vessels. It was the largest military force ever assembled at that point in history.

Greek cities faced an impossible choice: resist and face annihilation, or submit and survive as Persian subjects. Many chose submission. Thebes, one of the largest and most powerful cities in mainland Greece, *medized* (the Greek term for siding with Persia). The Thebans calculated that resistance was futile. Argos, another major city, stayed neutral. Thessaly and other northern regions submitted as the Persian army approached. Their location made resistance impractical. Even among those who chose to resist, many doubted Greece could win.

Only a coalition of cities, led by Sparta and Athens, was prepared to fight. But even this alliance was shaky. Cities squabbled over strategy and command. Southern cities wanted to defend only the Peloponnese and abandon everything north of the Isthmus of Corinth. Athens insisted on a forward defense. The Greeks were outnumbered, outmatched, and barely united.

The Greek strategy was born of desperation and cleverness in equal measure. They couldn't match Persia in open battle; the numbers were too lopsided. Instead, they would use Greece's geography as a weapon. Narrow mountain passes could negate the Persian numbers. Greek ships, which were heavier and better suited to close-quarters fighting, could contest Persian naval superiority in confined waters. The plan was to hold the Persians at chokepoints, buy time, and hope that Persian logistics would fail or that the invasion would lose momentum.

The first chokepoint was Thermopylae, a narrow coastal pass between the mountains and the sea in central Greece. The name means "Hot Gates," from the hot springs that bubbled up nearby. At its narrowest point, the pass was perhaps fifteen meters wide—just wide enough for a single cart with a little room on each side. An army trying to force the pass would have to attack in a narrow column, unable to deploy its full strength. A small force could hold it against a much larger one, at least for a while.

King Leonidas of Sparta led the Greek defense. The famous three hundred Spartans he brought were his personal guard. According to later tradition, they were all men with living sons who could inherit their family positions, though this detail might be an embellishment emphasizing their sacrifice. Leonidas certainly expected this to be a one-way mission. However, Leonidas also commanded about seven thousand other Greek soldiers from various cities: perhaps seven hundred from Thespiae, four hundred from Thebes, one thousand from Phocis, and contingents from Arcadia, Corinth, Mycenae, and other poleis. Ancient sources often focus on the three hundred Spartans because they make a better story, but the defense of Thermopylae was a panhellenic effort.

Leonidas at Thermopylae by Jacques-Louis David (1748–1825).[12]

The Greeks fortified the middle of the pass, where an old defensive wall already existed, rebuilding it to shoulder height. They positioned themselves to block the road and waited. When the Persian army arrived and spread across the plain south of the pass, it must have been a terrifying sight: thousands upon thousands of tents, campfires stretching to the horizon, and a constant noise of men, horses, and equipment.

Xerxes allegedly sent scouts to observe the Greek position. The scouts reported something baffling: the Spartans were exercising in the open and combing their long hair, seemingly unconcerned by the massive army confronting them. Xerxes consulted with Demaratus, an exiled Spartan king who accompanied the Persian court. Demaratus explained this was how Spartans prepared for battle. When they groomed themselves carefully, it meant they were ready to die. Xerxes still didn't believe a tiny force would actually fight.

Xerxes waited four days, apparently expecting the Greeks to flee once they fully grasped the hopelessness of their position. The Greeks didn't flee. On the fifth day, Xerxes's patience ran out. He ordered the attack.

The first assault was made by Medes and Cissians, troops from the empire's eastern regions. They advanced into the pass and discovered what it meant to fight Spartans in terrain that favored the phalanx. The Persians couldn't deploy their cavalry in the narrow pass. Their archers couldn't shoot effectively because the pass was too confined, and their own men blocked the field of fire. They had to advance in narrow columns directly into overlapping Greek shields and spears.

The Greek phalanx was designed for exactly this kind of fighting. Hoplites stood shoulder to shoulder, shields locked together, creating a bronze wall, spears protruding forward like a hedge of steel. Any Persian who got close enough to engage had to face multiple spear points at once while Greek shields blocked his weapons. The Persians couldn't outflank the phalanx because the mountains and sea hemmed them in. They could only push straight ahead and die on Greek spears.

The Persians attacked repeatedly throughout the day and were driven back with heavy casualties each time. Bodies piled up in the pass. Persian commanders reportedly whipped their men to force them forward into the killing ground. It didn't matter. The Greek position was too strong, their equipment too superior for this kind of fighting, and their discipline too solid to break under pressure.

On the second day, Xerxes sent forward his Immortals–the elite ten-thousand-man guard unit, the best troops in the Persian army. Surely they could break through where lesser troops had failed. They couldn't. The Immortals attacked and were repulsed like everyone else. According to Herodotus, the Spartans sometimes pretended to retreat in disorder, luring the Persians into pursuing them, and then suddenly wheeled around and slaughtered the disordered Persian troops. Whether this actually happened or is an embellishment, it represents the tactical sophistication the Spartans possessed. They didn't just hold their position; they fought intelligently.

By the end of the second day, thousands of Persians were dead, and the Greeks held firm. Xerxes had no solution. He reportedly jumped from his throne three times while watching the battle, terrified that his whole invasion would bog down at this single pass while winter approached.

Then came the betrayal. A local Greek man named Ephialtes came to Xerxes and offered to show the Persians a mountain path–the Anopaia trail–that led around the pass, allowing troops to descend behind the Greek position. Ephialtes was motivated by the promised reward and perhaps resentment at being left out of the fighting. Or maybe he simply calculated that Persia would win and wanted to be on the winning side. Whatever his reasons, his name became synonymous with betrayal in Greek culture. The Greek word *ephialtes* still means "nightmare."

The path was known to the Greeks. They'd posted Phocian soldiers to guard it. But the Phocians were surprised when the Persian forces, led by the Immortals, climbed the trail through the night. When the Persians came upon them at dawn, the Phocians didn't hold their ground and fight to the death. They withdrew to higher positions to defend their own territory rather than maintaining the critical path, and the Persians continued their descent toward the southern end of Thermopylae.

When Leonidas learned at dawn that the Persians were flanking his position, he knew the defensive position was lost. The Greek army was about to be caught between Persian forces in front and behind. He faced a grim choice. He could order a full retreat, saving most of his men but abandoning the pass and likely being harassed or destroyed during the withdrawal. Or he could hold the position as long as possible, buying time with lives.

Leonidas made a calculated decision. He ordered most of the Greek army to retreat and march south to the next defensive position. He and his three hundred Spartans would stay. The seven hundred Thespians, who came from a small city that chose honor over survival, refused to retreat and stayed with Leonidas. The four hundred Thebans were also still present. Their initial participation in the defense suggests some level of commitment, though later sources hostile to Thebes (which sided with Persia after Thermopylae) claim they remained unwillingly and eventually surrendered. The truth about the Thebans' actions is contested, but that is because it is complicated by later political animosity toward Thebes for medizing.

About 1,500 men, perhaps 2,000 at most, prepared for the last stand. They abandoned the defensive wall they'd been holding and moved forward to a wider part of the pass where they would have more room to fight in their final battle. This wasn't about holding a position anymore. This was about killing as many Persians as possible before dying and buying time for the rest of the Greek army to escape.

When the Persians attacked on the third day, the Greeks fought with suicidal fury. They knew they would die. The question was how many Persians they could take with them. They fought until their spears broke and then fought with swords. When their swords broke, Herodotus claims they fought with hands and teeth, though this may be a dramatic embellishment. What's certain is they fought with desperate courage, knowing no help was coming.

Leonidas fell early in the battle, and the fighting devolved into a savage struggle over his body. In Greek culture, recovering a fallen warrior's body for proper burial was a sacred duty. The Spartans fought ferociously to protect their king's corpse while the Persians fought equally hard to capture it as a trophy. Four times, according to Herodotus, the Spartans beat back the Persians and recovered Leonidas's body. Two of Xerxes's brothers died in this fighting.

Eventually, the Persian flanking force emerged from the mountain path behind them, and the last Greeks were surrounded. They retreated to a small hillock in the pass. Tradition says it's the hill that still exists there, though archaeologists debate this. The remaining Greeks climbed this hill and made their final stand.

The Persians surrounded the hill completely. By this point, they'd lost any desire to engage these maniacs in hand-to-hand combat. Persian commanders ordered their archers to simply shoot the Greeks down from a distance. Arrows fell like rain. The Greeks held their shields up and endured the storm as long as they could, but there were too many arrows from too many directions. One by one, the last defenders fell. Every Greek who had stayed with Leonidas died on that hill.

The Persians had won the battle. The pass was open. However, the cost had been enormous. There were thousands of Persian casualties, three days of brutal fighting to dislodge a tiny force, and the main Greek army had escaped intact to fight again. The Persians had lost time, momentum, and morale while learning that Greeks would fight to the death rather than submit.

More importantly, Thermopylae became legendary. The Greeks had lost, but it was a defeat that inspired people rather than demoralized them. The Spartans who stayed with Leonidas became the ultimate example of martial courage and devotion to duty. Soon after, a memorial was erected at Thermopylae with an inscription written by the poet Simonides: "Go tell the Spartans, stranger passing by, that here, obedient to their laws, we lie."

The message wasn't just about bravery. It was about citizenship, duty, and the willingness of free men to die for their polis and their laws. The Spartans at Thermopylae became a symbol of what Greeks were fighting for: the right to live under their own laws, in their own way, free from foreign domination. The battle was a military defeat, but it was a moral and psychological victory that unified Greek resistance.

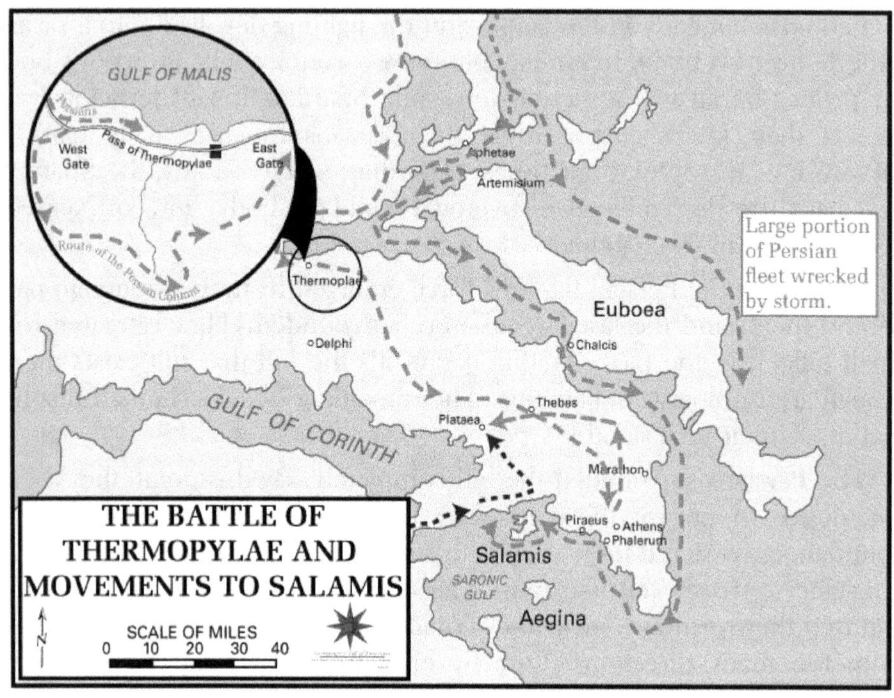

Major events in the second Persian invasion.[18]

While Leonidas and his men fought at Thermopylae, the Greek fleet engaged the Persian navy at Artemisium, a strait on the northern coast of Euboea. The timing was coordinated. The land army at Thermopylae and the fleet at Artemisium worked together to block both Persian routes into Greece.

The Greek fleet, commanded by the Spartan Eurybiades but dominated by Athenian ships under Themistocles, numbered perhaps 270 triremes. The Persian fleet was far larger—maybe six hundred to eight hundred warships initially, though storms had already damaged many. The Greeks chose Artemisium because the narrow waters negated the Persians' numerical advantage, just as the pass at Thermopylae neutralized their massive army.

For three days, the fleets clashed in the strait. The battles were brutal and exhausting. Greek triremes rammed Persian ships, marines fought on decks, and wreckage choked the waters. Neither side won decisively, but the Greeks inflicted significant damage on the Persian fleet and proved they could fight Persian ships effectively. More importantly, Athenian crews gained invaluable experience in naval combat—experience they would desperately need.

When news arrived that Thermopylae had fallen and the Persian army was marching south, the Greek fleet withdrew. There was no point holding Artemisium if the Persians controlled the pass behind them. The Greeks sailed south, shadowing the Persian advance, while Xerxes continued south with his vast army. Athens lay ahead, and behind it, the battles that would determine whether Greece would survive as a collection of free cities or become merely another province in the Persian Empire. But the Greeks had bought time at Thermopylae, and they would use that time well.

Triumph at Sea and Land: Salamis and Plataea

After Thermopylae, the Persian advance seemed unstoppable. The army marched south through Boeotia. Thebes and most other Boeotian cities welcomed them or offered no resistance. Nothing stood between Xerxes and Athens.

The Athenians couldn't defend their city against such an overwhelming force. In an extraordinary act of collective courage and desperation, they evacuated Athens entirely. The decision must have been wrenching. Athenians were abandoning their homes, temples, and ancestral lands—everything that defined them as a community. But they'd had warning and time to prepare.

Most refugees went to the nearby island of Salamis, visible from Athens across a narrow strait. Others went to Troezen in the Peloponnese, whose citizens generously agreed to shelter Athenian families. The Athenian fleet, which had been built up over the previous decade under Themistocles's urging, ferried people to safety. Women clutched children. Elderly citizens took what possessions they could carry. Families said goodbye to homes they'd never see again. Athens became a ghost town; it was eerily silent except for a small group of defenders who barricaded themselves on the Acropolis.

When the Persians arrived, they found the city nearly empty. They occupied Athens, climbed the Acropolis, and slaughtered the small group of defenders who had stayed. Then they burned everything. The temples went up in flames, including the predecessor to the Parthenon. The wooden structures burned quickly. Stone buildings were destroyed. Columns were toppled, and sculptures were smashed. This was revenge for Sardis, Marathon, and the Greeks' stubborn refusal to submit. Smoke from the burning city could be seen from Salamis, where Athenian refugees watched their home die.

But the Athenian fleet—roughly two hundred warships, almost half the total Greek navy, carrying most of Athens's fighting-age men—was intact and waiting in the narrow straits between Salamis and the mainland. The Greek allied fleet gathered at Salamis numbered perhaps 370 to 380 ships total. It was facing a Persian fleet that might have started with six hundred to eight hundred vessels but had been reduced by storms and previous naval skirmishes at Artemisium.

The question now was whether the Greeks would stay and fight or sail away to save what remained of their people and cities. The Athenians wanted to fight at Salamis. The straits were narrow—perfect for negating the Persian numerical advantage. But many other Greek commanders wanted to retreat to the Isthmus of Corinth and defend only the Peloponnese. From their perspective, Athens was already lost. Why risk the entire fleet trying to defend a burned city? Better to protect what could still be saved.

The council of war among Greek commanders grew heated. Themistocles, the Athenian leader who had convinced Athens to build its fleet, argued passionately that Salamis was where they had to make their stand. The narrow straits would work against the Persians just as Thermopylae's pass had worked for the Greeks on land. In confined waters, the heavier Greek triremes (warships with three banks of oars) would have the advantage. They could ram Persian ships and back away before being surrounded. Persian numbers wouldn't help them in tight quarters where they couldn't maneuver.

But Themistocles was losing the argument. The Spartan admiral and representatives from Corinth and other Peloponnesian cities insisted on retreating. The meeting broke up with no decision except to continue the debate the next day. Themistocles knew that if the debate continued, the Greeks would retreat and the Persian fleet would hunt them down in open water, where Persian numbers would be decisive.

So, Themistocles did something brilliantly devious. That night, he sent his slave Sicinnus secretly to the Persian camp with a message for Xerxes. The message claimed Themistocles was secretly a Persian sympathizer who wanted to help Xerxes win. It warned that the Greek fleet was planning to escape during the night and scatter in all directions. If Xerxes wanted to destroy the Greek navy, he should block the exits from the Salamis straits immediately and trap them.

Xerxes took the bait. He ordered his fleet to move during the night to block both exits from the strait. Egyptian ships blocked the western exit. Other Persian squadrons blocked the eastern exit and patrolled the strait itself. Persian marines landed on the small island of Psyttaleia in the middle of the strait to rescue Persian sailors or kill Greek sailors who ended up there. The Persians rowed all night, exhausting their crews, to spring the trap.

When dawn broke, Greek scouts reported that the Persians had them surrounded. The Greek commanders realized retreat was no longer an option. They would have to fight whether they wanted to or not. Themistocles had forced the battle he knew Greece needed.

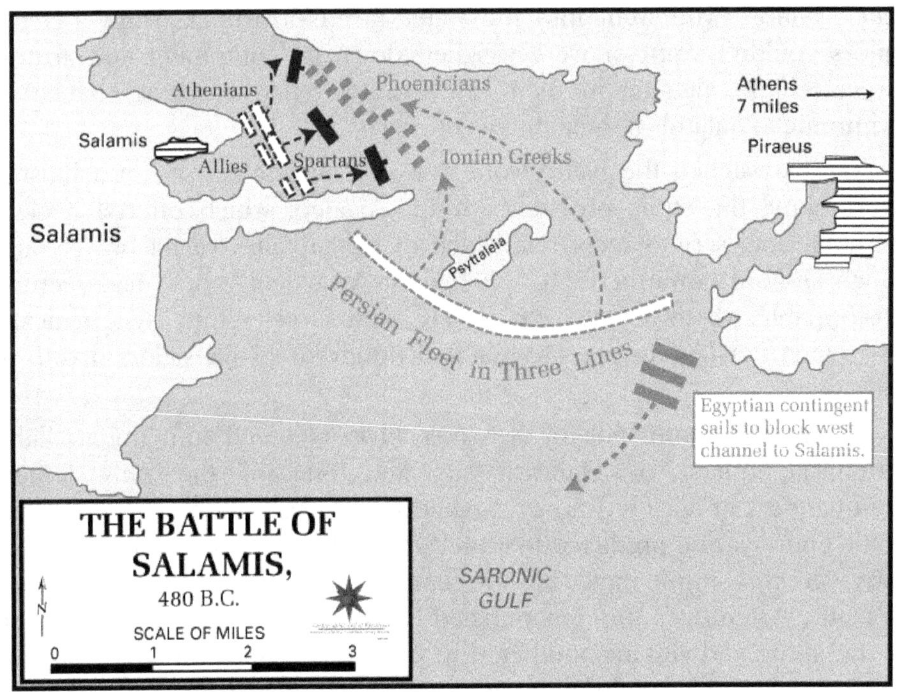

Movements in the Battle of Salamis.[14]

The Battle of Salamis began in the morning. The Persian fleet entered the narrows from the south, ship after ship filing into the confined space. This was precisely what Themistocles had wanted. The Persian ships, designed for fighting in open water where they could maneuver, found themselves crowded together in a space perhaps a mile wide. Ships collided with each other. Formations broke down. The Persian numerical advantage became a liability as hundreds of ships tried to operate in waters too narrow for them.

The Greek ships attacked aggressively. Greek triremes were heavier than most Persian vessels and sat lower in the water, making them more stable in rough seas and tight quarters. They had bronze rams on their prows designed to smash into enemy ships and crack their hulls below the waterline. Greek tactics were simple: row hard at an enemy ship, ram it, back away using oars, then repeat or move to the next target.

The battle quickly became chaotic and brutal. Greek ships drove into the mass of Persian vessels, ramming and then withdrawing before they could be surrounded. Persian ships couldn't deploy properly. They hit each other trying to maneuver. When a Greek trireme smashed into a Persian vessel and cracked its hull, the Persian ship would begin taking on water. Sailors who went into the water faced drowning. Many Persian sailors couldn't swim or were weighed down by equipment and armor. Greek sailors, fighting in their home waters, had a better chance of swimming to Salamis if their ship went down.

Xerxes watched the battle from a golden throne set up on a hillside overlooking the strait–probably Mount Aigaleo, which offered a clear view. He had scribes recording which of his captains fought bravely and which showed cowardice. He watched his vast fleet, which had seemed unstoppable, dissolve into chaos. He saw Greek ships systematically destroying Persian vessels. He watched hundreds of his sailors drown in the strait.

Before the battle, one of Xerxes's advisors urged him not to fight. Artemisia, queen of Halicarnassus and one of the only female commanders in ancient warfare, argued that Xerxes should avoid a naval battle entirely. She predicted that the Greek alliance would fracture on its own if Xerxes simply waited. Xerxes ignored her advice. During the chaos of battle, Artemisia's ship was pursued by Athenian triremes. She escaped by ramming and sinking another ship in Xerxes's fleet. Xerxes, watching from shore, saw the ramming and assumed she had sunk a Greek ship. He reportedly praised her courage, saying, "My men have become women, and my women have become men."

The battle raged for hours. Greek marines boarded damaged Persian ships and killed the crews. The waters of the strait turned red with blood.

By afternoon, the Persian fleet was shattered. Hundreds of ships had been sunk or damaged. Thousands of sailors were dead. The survivors fled back toward Phaleron Bay, where the main Persian fleet was anchored. The Greeks pursued but stopped short of a full-scale chase. They had won decisively and didn't want to risk everything by pursuing a still-dangerous enemy into open water.

The naval defeat changed Xerxes's strategic situation. Without naval supremacy, he couldn't safely supply his massive army through the winter. Every bite of food, every weapon, every piece of equipment had to come by land or sea from Asia. Greek control of the seas meant those supply lines were vulnerable. Winter was approaching. Keeping hundreds of thousands of men fed in hostile territory without secure sea lanes was impossible.

Xerxes made a crucial decision: he would return to Asia with much of his army, leaving his most capable general, Mardonius, with a picked force of perhaps fifty thousand to seventy thousand elite troops to continue the campaign the following spring. Mardonius would winter in friendly Thessaly and then complete the conquest of Greece when the campaigning season resumed.

The Greeks had won time. They'd proven that the Persians could be beaten at sea as decisively as they'd been beaten on land at Marathon. Xerxes's invasion, which had seemed unstoppable after Thermopylae, had been checked. However, the war wasn't over. A Persian army still occupied northern Greece, and Mardonius was one of Persia's best generals.

The following spring, in 479 BCE, the war reached its final climax. Mardonius, commanding the Persian force that had wintered in Thessaly and Boeotia, sent envoys to Athens with an offer. The message was simple and tempting. Athens had fought bravely, but continued resistance was pointless. If Athens were to switch sides and join Persia, it would be rewarded generously. Athens would be given land, autonomy, and favor. Persian money would rebuild the burned city. Athens would become Persia's privileged ally in Greece and would be given authority over other Greek cities.

It was a clever offer. Athens had already sacrificed everything. The city was destroyed, the population scattered, and the economy ruined. Continued fighting meant more suffering with no guarantee of victory. Accepting Persian terms meant peace, reconstruction, and prosperity. Many Athenians must have been tempted.

The Athenians refused. According to Herodotus, they told the Persian envoys that as long as the sun followed its current path in the sky, Athens would never make peace with Xerxes. They'd already lost their city once for freedom. They wouldn't trade that freedom now for Persian gold and empty promises of autonomy.

Mardonius's response was to march on Athens again. His army entered the already ruined city and burned what little remained standing. The Athenians evacuated to Salamis for the second time, watching their homes burn again. However, this time around, Sparta finally mobilized its full strength. The Spartans recognized that if Athens fell or switched sides, they would face Persia alone. So, they led the largest Greek army ever assembled north into Boeotia.

The Spartan regent Pausanias commanded perhaps forty thousand Greek hoplites plus tens of thousands of light troops (slaves and helots who served as skirmishers). The Greek force included contingents from dozens of cities, who were united in defense of their freedom. Against them, Mardonius commanded perhaps fifty thousand to seventy thousand troops, including Persian and Median cavalry and infantry, plus Greek allies like the Thebans who had chosen to support Persia.

The two armies met on the plain near Plataea, a small city at the edge of Theban territory. For more than a week, the armies maneuvered and skirmished without committing to a major battle. Mardonius had learned from Thermopylae. He wanted to fight on open ground where his cavalry could operate and where Persian archers could shower the Greeks with arrows. Pausanias wanted to fight on broken ground where the Greek phalanx would have the advantage and Persian cavalry would be less effective.

The stalemate dragged on. Persian cavalry harassed Greek supply lines and poisoned the Greeks' water source. The Greeks had to reposition during the night to find water and better ground. Mardonius, seeing the Greeks moving in the darkness, thought they were retreating in disorder and ordered an immediate attack. The Greeks were caught while still organizing their positions, their units scattered across the plain and not in proper formation.

A 19th-century illustration of the Battle of Plataea.[15]

What followed was the largest land battle of the Persian Wars and one of the largest battles in Greek history up to that point. The fighting was ferocious and desperate. On the Greek right, Spartan and Tegean hoplites faced the best Persian infantry. Pausanias, commanding the Spartans, held his position and prayed to the goddess Hera for victory while his men died around him. He refused to order the attack until the omens were right. It was either remarkable piety or battlefield psychology, making his men hold their ground under intense pressure while building their discipline and anger.

When Pausanias finally ordered the advance, the Spartans crashed into the Persian lines like a human avalanche. The Persian infantry fought bravely. They formed shield walls and shot arrows. But they weren't equipped or trained for this kind of close-quarters phalanx fighting. Greek hoplites with heavy armor, large shields, and long spears had every advantage in hand-to-hand combat. The Spartans pushed forward relentlessly.

Mardonius led his elite Persian troops from the front, fighting personally. According to Herodotus, a Spartan hoplite named Aristodemus killed Mardonius with a spear thrust, though other sources credit different Greek soldiers. What matters is that Mardonius died in the fighting. With their commander dead, Persian morale collapsed. The elite troops who had been holding against the Spartans broke and fled toward their fortified camp.

On other parts of the battlefield, Athenians and other Greeks were fighting Theban hoplites and other Greek medizers. These were Greeks fighting Greeks, which made it particularly bitter. The Athenians eventually drove the Thebans back, and the Greek phalanx began to converge on the Persian camp.

The Persians had built a wooden-walled fort as their base, and the survivors fled there seeking protection. The walls should have been a strong defensive position. However, walls meant nothing to Greeks who'd fought through the narrow pass at Thermopylae and stood against impossible odds. The Greeks stormed the fortifications, broke through the wooden walls, and poured into the camp. What followed was a massacre. The trapped Persian soldiers were cut down by the thousands. Few escaped. The Persian army that was supposed to conquer Greece was annihilated.

Greek casualties were significant. Herodotus reports that 159 Spartans, 52 Athenians, and 16 Tegeans were killed, though other cities suffered losses too. Persian losses were catastrophic; tens of thousands died in the battle and the subsequent slaughter in the camp.

On the same day—or so later Greeks claimed, and the coincidence was too perfect to be accidental, even if not literally true—the Greek fleet won another decisive victory at Mycale on the coast of Asia Minor. Greek ships, emboldened by Salamis, crossed the Aegean and attacked the beached Persian fleet. The Greeks landed their marines, defeated the Persian force defending the ships, and burned the Persian fleet where it sat. The Ionian cities, seeing Persian power broken, revolted again and this time successfully joined the Greek alliance.

The Persian invasion was over. Xerxes's dream of conquering Greece had died in the waters of Salamis and on the field of Plataea. The Persian army limped back to Asia. Many Greek cities in Asia Minor broke free from Persian control in the immediate aftermath, though this "liberation" would prove temporary and uneven. Persian influence in the region would continue for decades, and complete independence would only come much later. Still, the vast empire that had seemed unstoppable had been checked by a coalition of independent cities that loved their freedom more than they feared death.

The Persian Wars ended in an astonishing, unlikely Greek victory. The Greeks faced a superpower that controlled territory from Egypt to India. They had won through courage, clever tactics, and willingness to sacrifice everything rather than submit to foreign rule. Greeks learned that their way of life, with its squabbling cities, its contentious assemblies, and its emphasis on individual achievement, could triumph over the organized might of eastern despotism.

But victory came at enormous cost. Athens was destroyed twice. Greek casualties across multiple battles numbered in the thousands. The Greek world had been devastated by invasion. Alliances formed during the war created new tensions, and the experience of fighting together had changed the balance of power among Greek cities in ways that would have profound consequences.

Athens emerged from the war as a major power. The Athenian navy had been crucial at Salamis and Mycale. The Athenians' sacrifice earned them respect and influence. Sparta's military reputation was confirmed and enhanced. The coalition had saved Greece, but the alliance was fragile and built on temporary shared interests rather than a lasting friendship.

Seeds of future conflict had been planted. Athens and Sparta had cooperated to defeat Persia, but they had fundamentally different visions for what Greece should become. Athens would use its naval power to build an empire. Sparta would resist Athenian expansion. The Persian Wars were over, but the Greek wars against each other were just beginning.

Chapter 6 – The Golden Age and the Great War

Building an Empire: The Delian League

The Persian Wars ended in 479 BCE with a Greek victory, but the question of what came next divided the Greek world almost immediately. Sparta wanted to go home. The Spartans had done their part; they'd led the defense of Greece, their hoplites had broken the Persian army at Plataea, and now they wanted to return to the Peloponnese and resume their lives. Sparta had no interest in foreign adventures or overseas commitments. The helots back home were restless, and Spartan citizens were needed to maintain control there.

Athens saw things differently. The Persians had been driven from mainland Greece, but the threat wasn't over. Persian forces still controlled or threatened Greek cities in Asia Minor and the Aegean islands. The Persian navy, though badly damaged, still existed. Xerxes still sat on his throne in Persia, and there was no guarantee he wouldn't try again. Athens argued that the Greeks needed to stay on the offensive. They should liberate the Greek cities still under Persian control, protect Greece against future invasions, and make Persia pay for what they'd done. The formal war would continue for decades, with a peace treaty not concluded until around 449 BCE, according to most modern historians.

Athens had another motivation that wasn't purely altruistic. The city had been destroyed twice during the war. The Athenian economy was in ruins. Rebuilding would be expensive, and Athens needed money.

Control of the Aegean Sea and the trade routes that crossed it could make Athens wealthy. Leadership of an anti-Persian alliance would give Athens power and influence. The opportunity to transform Athens from a regional power into something much greater was there for the taking.

Sparta initially tried to maintain leadership of the Greek alliance. The Spartan regent Pausanias, the victor of Plataea, led a Greek fleet in 478 BCE to liberate Greek cities in Cyprus and Byzantium. However, Pausanias's leadership was disastrous. He was arrogant and autocratic, allegedly adopting Persian dress and manners. He offended the allied commanders and alienated the cities he was supposed to be liberating. Rumors spread that he was conspiring with Persia. Whether the accusations were true or not—they might have been at least partially Athenian propaganda—Sparta recalled Pausanias and essentially withdrew from overseas leadership.

This created a vacuum that Athens eagerly filled. In 478/477 BCE, Athens organized a new alliance specifically dedicated to continuing the war against Persia. The alliance would be called the Delian League, named after the island of Delos, where the league's treasury was kept and where representatives met. It would become one of the most successful and controversial alliances in Greek history.

The structure of the Delian League seemed fair and reasonable on paper. Member cities would contribute either ships and crews to the allied fleet or money to pay for ships if they couldn't provide them directly. Athens, with the largest navy in Greece, would command the fleet. Aristides, an Athenian statesman known for his fairness and honesty, assessed each member's contribution based on their wealth and resources. No one could accuse Aristides of unfairness; he was so respected that Athenians nicknamed him "the Just."

The league's stated purpose was to liberate Greek cities from Persian control, protect against future Persian aggression, and punish Persia for the invasion by raiding Persian territory. Every member city swore an oath of alliance, and lumps of iron were thrown into the sea, symbolizing that the alliance would last until the iron floated, meaning forever.

Initially, the Delian League worked exactly as advertised. Under Athenian leadership, particularly under the general Cimon (son of Miltiades, the hero of Marathon), the league achieved spectacular successes. Greek cities in Asia Minor and along the Thracian coast were liberated from Persian control. The league's fleet hunted down Persian ships and destroyed them. In the 460s BCE, Cimon led a major expedition to the Eurymedon River in Asia Minor and won a stunning double victory, destroying the Persian fleet and then landing troops to defeat the Persian army on the same day.

These victories were significant. Cities that had lived under Persian rule for decades were freed, and the Persian threat to the Aegean was pushed back. The league was accomplishing its mission. Athens genuinely was the liberator and protector it claimed to be.

But things changed gradually. The nature of the alliance began to shift in ways that benefited Athens at the expense of other members. More and more cities chose to contribute money rather than ships. This made sense for small cities since building and maintaining a trireme warship was expensive, and manning it required 170 rowers. It was easier to pay Athens to provide the ships. However, this meant that Athens controlled an ever-larger fleet while other cities had no ships of their own.

Athens, meanwhile, used the money not just to build warships but also to pay Athenian rowers. This created jobs for thousands of Athenian citizens, particularly the poorer classes who rowed the ships. The fleet became an economic engine for Athens. Athenian power and prosperity depended on the league's continued existence and expansion. Moreover, the empire secured vital grain imports from the Black Sea region; Athens couldn't feed its population from Attic farmland alone. Control of the sea lanes meant survival. The tribute also funded the payments that allowed poorer citizens to serve on juries and attend the Assembly, making Athenian democracy feasible for all citizens, not just the wealthy who could afford to participate in politics without compensation. The empire and Athenian democracy became inseparable–one sustained the other.

The league also began to serve Athenian interests beyond just fighting Persia. When the island of Naxos tried to withdraw from the league around 470 BCE, Athens responded with force. Naxos was besieged, forced back into the league, and punished. Its walls were torn down. The message was clear: you couldn't leave the league. What had been presented as a voluntary alliance was becoming compulsory.

The Athenian historian Thucydides, writing decades later, identified this as the moment when the league's nature fundamentally changed. Naxos was "the first allied city to be enslaved contrary to established usage," he wrote. The word "enslaved" is harsh but telling. Cities that had joined freely to fight Persia were now being forced to stay in an alliance whose purpose was increasingly unclear.

Other cities that tried to leave were similarly crushed. Thasos revolted in 465 BCE over a dispute about trade and mining rights—nothing to do with Persia—and Athens besieged the city for two years until it surrendered. Thasos lost its fleet, had to pay a huge indemnity, and effectively became a subject of Athens. The pattern repeated with other cities. Rebellion meant siege, defeat, punishment, and loss of autonomy.

In 454 BCE, Athens moved the league's treasury from Delos to Athens itself. The official reason was security; keeping the treasury on a small island was risky. However, the real reason was control. With the treasury in Athens, the Athenians could access the money directly. They began using league funds for Athenian purposes. The massive building program that would create the Parthenon and beautify Athens was likely funded in part by league contributions. Direct documentation doesn't survive, but the circumstantial evidence and contemporary political complaints strongly suggest this.

The allies protested, but they were powerless to stop it. Pericles, Athens's dominant political figure by the 440s BCE, dismissed the complaints. As long as Athens protected the allies from Persia, he argued, how Athens spent the money was Athens's business. If the allies didn't like it, they could build their own fleets and defend themselves. Of course, Athens wouldn't let them do that either.

By the mid-century, the Delian League had transformed into something its founders probably hadn't intended: an Athenian empire. Athens controlled the league absolutely. Member cities, which counted well over a hundred at the empire's height, with numbers fluctuating around 150to 200 based on surviving tribute records, had to follow Athenian foreign policy. They had to use Athenian weights, measures, and coinage. Serious legal cases from allied cities were heard in Athenian courts under Athenian law by Athenian jurors. Athens sometimes installed garrisons in allied cities or established colonies of Athenian citizens in allied territory. The allies had to pay tribute; yes, the word changed from "contributions" to "tribute," which tells you everything about how the relationship had evolved.

This imperial system was enormously profitable for Athens. Money flowed into the city from hundreds of allied or subject cities. This wealth funded everything that made 5th-century Athens remarkable: the building programs, the dramatic festivals, the payments to citizens for jury service and attending the Assembly, and the fleet that made Athens the greatest naval power in the Mediterranean.

The Athenians themselves were remarkably honest about this transformation. Pericles, in a famous speech recorded by Thucydides, acknowledged that "your empire is now like a tyranny: it may have been wrong to take it, but it is certainly dangerous to let it go." The Athenians knew they were running an empire. And they knew their allies resented them. Many Athenians accepted these costs as the price of Athenian greatness and security, prioritizing power and prosperity over popularity with their subjects. The empire made Athens great, and for most Athenians, that justified the resentment it created.

However, not all Athenians were comfortable with this. Some worried about the moral implications of ruling other Greeks by force. The playwright Euripides wrote plays that questioned Athenian imperialism. Thucydides himself, though he admired Athenian power, was clearly troubled by what Athens had become. Most Athenians didn't seem to notice or care about the contradiction. They celebrated democracy at home while denying it to their subjects abroad. They praised freedom while forcing other Greeks to obey Athenian commands.

From the perspective of the subject allies, Athens had betrayed the league's founding principles. They'd joined voluntarily to fight Persia and protect Greek freedom. Now they were subjects of an Athenian empire, paying tribute, losing autonomy, and seeing their money spent on Athenian projects while they lacked a voice in how the alliance operated. To be fair, some allies did benefit. Athenian naval power protected trade routes, suppressed piracy, and provided security against Persian resurgence. Smaller cities gained stability they couldn't have achieved alone. However, these benefits came at the cost of independence, and for many Greeks, freedom mattered more than security. The great liberator had become an oppressor, or at least a domineering protector who demanded obedience in exchange for protection.

Other Greek states watched this transformation with alarm. Sparta had stayed largely out of Aegean affairs since withdrawing from overseas leadership, but the growth of Athenian power was impossible to ignore. By the 440s and 430s BCE, Athens had become the richest and most powerful Greek state, commanding hundreds of ships and collecting tribute from hundreds of cities. This was a dramatic shift in the balance of power.

Corinth, a major commercial power and a Spartan ally, was particularly worried. Athenian trade and Athenian colonies were competing with Corinthian interests throughout the Greek world. Thebes, which dominated Boeotia, resented Athenian interference in central Greece. Even states that had fought alongside Athens against Persia began to fear Athenian ambitions.

The irony was profound. Greece had united, however imperfectly, to defend its freedom against Persian imperialism. Now, barely a generation later, an Athenian empire was dominating the Aegean, and Greeks were preparing to fight Greeks over whether Athens should be allowed to continue its imperial expansion. The victory over Persia had saved Greek independence, but it had also created conditions for Greece's self-destruction.

For now, though, in the mid-5th century BCE, Athens stood at its peak. The Persian threat had receded. Tribute flowed in from across the Aegean. The fleet ruled the seas. The city was being rebuilt in marble rather than wood, with monuments that would last millennia. Democracy was flourishing. Culture was exploding in new directions. This was Athens's moment of greatest power and achievement–what later generations would call the golden age.

Democracy's Flowering: Pericles and Athens

If you could visit Athens in the 440s and 430s BCE, you'd find a city unlike anywhere else in the Greek world or anywhere in the world, for that matter. Athens in its golden age was loud, chaotic, argumentative, and gloriously alive with political energy. On Assembly days and when the courts were in session, thousands of citizens gathered in the agora to argue about politics, listen to speeches, serve on juries, or conduct business. The city hummed with debate, gossip, lawsuits, and democratic participation on a scale that would have seemed insane to most ancient peoples, though in practice, many citizens lived in rural Attica and couldn't attend regularly, meaning active political participation was more feasible for those living in or near the city itself.

At the center of this energy, for nearly three decades, stood Pericles. He wasn't a king, tyrant, or dictator. He held no permanent office and could be voted out at any time. But he was elected strategos–one of ten generals–fifteen times over his career continuously from 443 BCE until his death in 429 BCE (with one exception when he was briefly removed from office in 430 BCE). He used this position to guide Athenian policy, champion democracy, and transform Athens into the cultural capital of Greece.

A bust of Pericles.[16]

Pericles came from an aristocratic family. His mother was a member of the Alcmaeonid clan, one of Athens's most powerful families. His father Xanthippus had commanded the Greek fleet at Mycale. According to later ancient sources, Pericles received the best education available, studying with the philosopher Anaxagoras and learning rhetoric from the sophist Protagoras. He was wealthy, well connected, and brilliant–exactly the sort of person who in an earlier era would have competed with other aristocrats for power.

But Pericles chose a different path. He became a champion of democracy and positioned himself as a leader of the demos, or the common people. This wasn't entirely altruistic. Athenian politics had roughly two factions: the aristocratic conservatives, who wanted to limit democracy and maintain traditional elite privileges, and the democratic radicals, who wanted to expand citizen participation and reduce aristocratic power. Pericles allied himself with the democrats, recognizing that his path to power ran through popular support rather than aristocratic backing.

Under Pericles's leadership, Athenian democracy reached its fullest development. Cleisthenes had created the basic democratic structure a generation earlier, but Pericles expanded and deepened it. His reforms made democracy functional for all citizens, not just those wealthy enough to spend time on politics without compensation.

The most important reform attributed to Pericles was the introduction of pay for jury service. Before this, serving on juries meant losing a day's wages. Poor citizens couldn't afford to participate regularly. This meant that in practice, the courts were dominated by the wealthy who had leisure time. Pericles introduced payment for jury service (*misthos*), allowing poor citizens to serve without suffering economic hardship. Payment for attending the Assembly would come later, likely around 400 BCE, after Pericles's death.

Critics, particularly wealthy conservatives, were horrified. They argued that paying citizens for jury service would attract the wrong sort of people: lazy men looking for easy money rather than serious citizens devoted to justice. They worried that poor citizens would become too dependent on state payments and vote for politicians who promised them more benefits. Some conservatives sarcastically called the payments "the sophist's wage," implying that citizens were being bribed to pretend to care about their civic duties.

But Pericles argued that democracy meant rule by all citizens, not just those who could afford time off. If citizens were expected to serve the state by fighting in the army, rowing in the fleet, and serving on juries, then the state should compensate them fairly. The wealthy could afford to serve for free; the poor couldn't. Payment leveled the playing field, at least in the courts.

The Athenian Assembly met on the Pnyx, a hill west of the Acropolis. About forty times a year, thousands of citizens would gather to debate and vote on laws, declarations of war, treaties, budgets, and every other major decision. For certain particularly important matters, such as ostracism or grants of citizenship, a quorum of six thousand citizens was required, though ordinary business could proceed with fewer. Any citizen could speak, though in practice, trained orators dominated the debates. Anyone could propose a law. Every citizen had one vote, and it counted equally whether he was rich or poor, educated or illiterate, aristocrat or laborer.

The Assembly was chaotic and rowdy. Citizens shouted approval or disapproval during speeches. They heckled speakers they disliked. They laughed at jokes and booed bad arguments. Voting was usually by a show of hands, though important decisions might use a secret ballot. The atmosphere was more like a sports event than a modern legislature.

Juries were even more democratic and more unusual by ancient standards. Athenian juries were massive, typically consisting of 201 or 501 citizens, sometimes more for important cases. Jurors were selected by lot each day from volunteers. Any citizen over thirty could volunteer. This meant that a trial might be decided by hundreds of ordinary Athenians with no legal training, chosen at random that morning.

There were no judges in the modern sense, and there were no professional lawyers, prosecutors, or defense attorneys. The plaintiff and defendant represented themselves, delivering timed speeches explaining their case. Each side could call witnesses. After hearing both sides, jurors voted on guilt or innocence. If the defendant was found guilty and the penalty wasn't fixed by law, there would be a second round of voting to determine the punishment, with both sides proposing penalties and the jury choosing between them. There was no appeal. The majority ruled, and the decision was final.

This system seems crazy by modern standards. How could untrained citizens make complex legal decisions? How could justice be served when juries were essentially mobs of random people? But Athenians believed this was exactly the point. The law shouldn't be a mystery understood only by experts. Justice shouldn't be decided by a small elite. The community as a whole should determine guilt or innocence, and punishments should reflect community values.

Athenians were litigation-happy. Thousands of cases came before the courts each year—disputes over property, contracts, inheritances, assault, theft, and especially political prosecutions. Athenian politicians regularly sued each other, using the courts as an arena for political combat. This meant that persuasive rhetoric mattered enormously. If you could convince a jury, you won. If you couldn't, you lost, even if the law and facts were on your side.

This created demand for teachers of rhetoric—the sophists—who charged fees to teach wealthy young men how to argue persuasively. Critics complained that sophists taught students to make the weaker argument appear stronger and to win through verbal trickery rather than truth. The philosopher Socrates was famously suspicious of sophistic rhetoric and the Athenian love of persuasive speaking over genuine wisdom.

Pericles himself was a masterful orator. Ancient sources describe him as dignified, reserved, and extraordinarily persuasive. He didn't shout or gesture wildly like some politicians. He spoke with careful, measured authority that commanded attention. The comic playwright Aristophanes joked that Pericles wielded "the lightning and thunder of Zeus" with his speeches. When Pericles spoke in the Assembly, people listened.

His most famous speech, or at least the most famous speech Thucydides attributes to him, was the Funeral Oration, delivered in 431 BCE to honor Athenians who died in the first year of the Peloponnesian War. Thucydides's version of this speech (we don't have Pericles's actual words, only Thucydides's reconstruction) has become one of the most celebrated statements of democratic values in Western literature.

In the speech, Pericles celebrated Athens as a model for all Greece. "Our constitution is called a democracy because power is in the hands not of a minority but of the whole people," he declared. Athens didn't copy other cities; other cities copied Athens. Athenians were free to live as they pleased and were encouraged to debate and disagree. They valued beauty without extravagance, wisdom without softness, and wealth as an opportunity for action rather than for boasting.

The speech was brilliant propaganda. It defined Athens by its values—freedom, openness, courage, and culture—rather than by its power. It claimed moral superiority for democracy over other systems. It assured grieving families that their loved ones had died for the greatest city in the world, defending principles worth dying for.

But the speech was also honest about what Athens had become. Pericles acknowledged that Athens ruled an empire "like a tyranny," but argued this was necessary and justified. He celebrated Athenian power openly. Athens didn't need Homer to sing its praises; Athens's achievements spoke for themselves. The speech captured the confidence, bordering on arrogance, of Athens at its peak.

Under Pericles, Athens also became physically beautiful. The massive building program that created the Parthenon and other monuments on the Acropolis was Pericles's vision. Before the Persian Wars, the Acropolis had temples and sacred buildings. The Persians destroyed them all. For thirty years, the ruins remained, a deliberate reminder of Persian sacrilege and Athenian sacrifice.

Pericles decided Athens should rebuild but not just restore what was lost. Athens would build monuments worthy of the greatest city in Greece, temples that would last forever, built in marble instead of wood, decorated by the finest sculptors, and designed by the best architects. The Parthenon, dedicated to Athena, would be the centerpiece: thirty feet tall, surrounded by forty-six massive columns, decorated with intricate sculptural friezes showing battles, processions, and mythological scenes. It would be beautiful, awe-inspiring, and a permanent statement of Athenian power and culture.

The Parthenon.[17]

Critics attacked the building program as wasteful vanity. Thucydides (a different Thucydides, not the historian) accused Pericles of "dressing Athens up like a harlot" with expensive jewelry while allied cities suffered. The money came from tribute, so it should be spent on defense, not on making Athens pretty.

Pericles's response was unapologetic. As long as Athens defended the allies, how Athens spent the money was Athens's business. Besides, the building program employed thousands of Athenian artisans, sculptors, laborers, carpenters, and painters. It enriched the city economically and culturally. Centuries from now, people would look at these monuments and know Athens had been great. He was right about that.

The Parthenon was completed in 438 BCE, with the sculptural decorations finished a few years later. It stood—and still stands, though damaged—as the ultimate symbol of Athens's golden age. When ancient travelers listed the wonders of the world, Athens's monuments were celebrated alongside the pyramids of Giza and the Hanging Gardens of Babylon. The Parthenon represented Athenian democracy, culture, imperialism, and confidence all in one massive marble structure.

But Athenian democracy, for all its achievements, had severe limitations that Pericles never addressed and probably never questioned. Democracy was only for citizens, and citizenship was restricted. Women couldn't participate in politics, hold office, or vote. They couldn't own property in their own names or represent themselves in court. Upper-class women lived secluded lives, rarely appearing in public. They managed households but had no public role. Working-class women had more freedom by necessity. They worked as vendors, midwives, and weavers, but they still had no political rights.

Slaves were everywhere in Athens. Perhaps one-third of Athens's population was enslaved. They worked in homes, workshops, mines, and fields. Some were treated relatively well, working alongside free laborers and sometimes earning enough to eventually buy their freedom. Others, particularly those working in the silver mines at Laurium, endured brutal conditions and short lives. Democracy depended on slave labor to function. Citizens had time for politics in part because enslaved people did much of the work.

Metics—foreign residents—could live and work in Athens, sometimes for generations, but could never become citizens, no matter how long they stayed or how much they contributed to the city. They paid taxes, fought in the army, and participated in the economy, but they had no political voice. Citizenship was hereditary and jealously guarded. In 451 BCE, Pericles himself sponsored a law requiring that both parents be Athenian citizens for their children to be citizens, further restricting who counted as Athenian.

So, when Pericles celebrated "democracy" and "rule by the people," he meant rule by perhaps 40,000 to 60,000 adult male citizens out of a total population of perhaps 300,000 to 400,000 people. The majority of people living in Athens had no political rights at all.

Modern critics point out this hypocrisy, and they're right to do so. Athenian democracy was deeply exclusionary. But we should also recognize that by ancient standards, Athens was radical. No other major city allowed anything like this level of participation, even for its citizens. Most were oligarchies where a few dozen or a few hundred wealthy men controlled everything. Athens gave political power to tens of thousands of ordinary men who would have had no voice anywhere else.

Cultural Explosion: Drama, Philosophy, and Art

While Athenian politicians debated in the Assembly and generals commanded fleets, Athens was experiencing an explosion of cultural creativity that would influence Western civilization for millennia. The same decades that saw the building of the Parthenon also produced revolutionary developments in drama, philosophy, sculpture, and art. Athens in the 5th century BCE wasn't just politically innovative; it was also culturally transformative.

The heart of Athenian cultural life was theater, and theater was deeply connected to democracy and civic religion. Twice a year, during festivals honoring the god Dionysus, Athens held dramatic competitions. The City Dionysia in spring was the major event. For several days, thousands of Athenians gathered in the Theatre of Dionysus on the slope of the Acropolis to watch plays.

These weren't optional entertainment for those who could afford tickets. Theater was a civic duty, a religious observance, and a shared community experience all at once. Productions were funded through a combination of state support and private sponsorship. Wealthy citizens were assigned as *choregos*–sponsors who bore most of the production costs as a form of public service (and competition for prestige), while the state covered certain expenses like actors' pay. Metics likely attended as well, as well as possibly some slaves and foreigners, though evidence for non-citizen attendance is limited.

Greek theater had two main forms: tragedy and comedy. Tragedies dealt with serious themes, like fate, justice, the relationship between humans and gods, and the consequences of hubris and moral choices. They drew heavily on mythology, retelling familiar stories but exploring their deeper meanings and moral complexities. Comedies were satirical, bawdy, politically sharp, and often hilarious, mocking politicians, philosophers, social trends, and Athens itself.

The three great tragedians whose works survive are Aeschylus, Sophocles, and Euripides. Each brought something different to the form and pushed Greek drama in new directions.

Aeschylus, who fought at Marathon and possibly Salamis, was the earliest of the three. His plays explored grand cosmic themes like justice, divine will, and the cycle of revenge and redemption. His masterpiece, the *Oresteia* trilogy, tells the story of Agamemnon's murder by his wife Clytemnestra and the subsequent revenge by their son Orestes. The trilogy ends with the establishment of the Athenian court system, transforming the cycle of blood revenge into civilized justice. It's both a thrilling story and a meditation on how societies move from barbarism to law. Aeschylus died in 456 BCE, but his plays continue to be celebrated today.

Sophocles dominated Athenian theater for much of the 5th century. He won first prize at the City Dionysia approximately twenty times and reportedly never finished lower than second. His plays focused on individual characters facing impossible moral dilemmas. *Oedipus the King* tells the story of a man who unknowingly killed his father and married his mother, then desperately tried to uncover the truth even as everyone warned him to stop asking questions. It's a devastating exploration of fate, knowledge, and the limits of human understanding. *Antigone* examines the conflict between divine law and human law and between family duty and civic obligation through a young woman who defies the king to bury her brother.

Sophocles's characters feel psychologically real in ways that ancient literature rarely achieved. They struggle with doubt, make mistakes, suffer consequences, and endure. His plays don't provide easy moral answers; they present genuinely difficult choices where doing the right thing leads to disaster. This moral complexity reflected the complexities of democratic Athens, where citizens constantly faced difficult decisions about justice, duty, and the common good.

Euripides was the most controversial and psychologically daring of the three. His plays questioned traditional values, explored the darker aspects of human nature, and gave powerful voices to women and slaves–people who had no voice in Athenian politics. *Medea* tells the story of a foreign woman who murders her own children to punish her unfaithful husband. It's horrifying, but Euripides makes you understand Medea's rage and betrayal. *The Trojan Women*, produced in 415 BCE during the Peloponnesian War, depicts the aftermath of the fall of Troy from the perspective of the conquered women. It's a powerful anti-war statement that questioned Athenian imperialism when Athens was at war and conquering other cities.

Euripides wasn't as popular as Sophocles during his lifetime (he only won first prize five times), but his psychological realism and willingness to challenge conventional morality influenced later drama enormously. He died in 406 BCE, and the Athenians, who had often been uncomfortable with his plays, mourned him deeply.

Comedy was different. It was louder, ruder, and more directly political. The greatest comic playwright was Aristophanes. His plays were crude, vulgar, and brutally funny, mocking politicians, philosophers, and generals without mercy. Nothing was off-limits.

In *The Knights*, he portrayed the Athenian demos (the people) as a senile old man being manipulated by a sleazy politician. In *The Clouds*, he savagely satirized Socrates as a sophist who taught students to make bad arguments sound good and to cheat their creditors. In *Lysistrata*, the women of Greece go on a sex strike to force their husbands to end the Peloponnesian War. The play is hilarious, sexually explicit, and also a serious meditation on war's costs.

Aristophanes could get away with this because Athenian democracy tolerated and even encouraged criticism and mockery. You could stand in the Theatre of Dionysus and watch a play that brutally mocked the generals, the Assembly, and the whole democratic system performed at a state-sponsored festival. This was freedom of speech in action. It was messy, uncomfortable, and vital.

While playwrights explored human nature through drama, philosophers were developing new ways of thinking about the world, knowledge, and morality. The intellectual revolution happening in Athens would reshape Western thought.

Earlier Greek philosophers had already been asking radical questions about the nature of reality, and many, including some sophists and pre-Socratic thinkers, had engaged with ethics, human knowledge, and society. But 5th-century Athens saw philosophy become more intensely focused on human concerns, like ethics, politics, knowledge, and how to live a good life. The sophists, professional teachers who charged fees, taught rhetoric, debate, and practical wisdom to wealthy young men. Some sophists seemed to argue that truth was relative and that persuasive speech mattered more than actual virtue; in other words, that might made right. Critics worried they were teaching cynical manipulation rather than genuine wisdom.

Then came Socrates. He didn't write anything down. Everything we know about him comes from his students and contemporaries, particularly Plato and Xenophon, who provide different but complementary perspectives on his life and teachings. Socrates transformed philosophy by making it a matter of constant questioning rather than providing answers. He wandered around Athens engaging anyone who would talk with him in philosophical dialogue, asking seemingly simple questions that revealed how little people actually understood about concepts they took for granted. What is justice? What is courage? What is virtue? When people gave confident answers, Socrates would ask follow-up questions until their certainty crumbled and they realized they didn't really know what they were talking about.

This made him deeply annoying to many Athenians, but Socrates believed this questioning was essential. The unexamined life, he famously said, is not worth living. You couldn't live ethically if you hadn't thought carefully about what ethics meant. Conventional answers weren't good enough. You had to understand why things were right or wrong, not just accept what society told you.

Socrates insisted that virtue was knowledge. If you truly understood what was good, you would do it. People only did wrong because they were confused or ignorant about what was actually good for them. This was a radical idea that suggested moral education was possible and essential.

Socrates also questioned democracy, which didn't make him popular. In Plato's writings, Socrates uses the analogy of governing being like sailing a ship. You wouldn't let just anyone steer, regardless of whether they knew how. Why, then, should anyone be allowed to vote on complex political matters regardless of whether they understood them? Shouldn't governance require expertise? This critique of democracy, as presented by Plato, would influence political philosophy for centuries, though it didn't prevent Socrates from staying in Athens and obeying its laws (mostly).

Socrates would eventually be executed by Athens in 399 BCE on charges of impiety and corrupting the youth. Whether this was a legitimate claim or political persecution remains debated. His student Plato would carry on his philosophical project, founding the Academy and writing dialogues that preserved Socratic questioning while developing a comprehensive philosophical system.

Plato's student Aristotle would study at the Academy and then found his own school, the Lyceum. Between them, Socrates, Plato, and Aristotle would create the foundation of Western philosophy. This all took place in Athens, all within a span of about a century.

While philosophers questioned and playwrights explored, sculptors were revolutionizing how humans depicted the body. Earlier Greek sculpture had been stiff and stylized, with the "archaic smile" and rigid poses of *kouroi* (standing male statues). But 5th-century sculptors achieved something unprecedented: they made marble look alive.

The sculptor Myron created bronze statues like the *Discus Thrower* that captured bodies in motion with perfect anatomical accuracy. Polykleitos wrote a treatise on ideal proportions and created statues like the *Doryphoros* (Spear-Bearer) that embodied his mathematical approach to representing the perfect human form. These weren't just technically skillful; they were also beautiful, capturing both physical perfection and an idealized human dignity.

A Roman copy of the Discus Thrower.[18]

Phidias is widely considered the greatest sculptor of the age. He served as chief artistic director for the Parthenon's sculptural program. The temple's pediments, metopes, and frieze were filled with sculptures depicting mythological battles, the birth of Athena, and a grand procession of Athenian citizens. These sculptures showed figures in complex poses, with flowing drapery that revealed the body beneath, faces that conveyed emotion, and compositions that made the stone seem to move.

Phidias also created the statue of Athena Parthenos that stood inside the Parthenon. It was nearly forty feet tall, made of gold and ivory, and showed the goddess in full armor. It was one of the most famous statues in the ancient world, though it no longer survives. He later created an even more famous statue of Zeus at Olympia, which was considered one of the Seven Wonders of the Ancient World.

A Roman copy of Phidias's Athena. It is thought to be the most faithful reproduction of this work.[19]

Greek sculpture from this period influenced art for the next 2,500 years. Renaissance artists studied Greek proportions and poses. Neoclassical sculptors tried to recreate Greek ideals. Even today, our ideas about how to represent the human body in art owe an enormous debt to 5th-century Athenian sculptors.

Painting was also flourishing, though almost none of it survives. We know from ancient descriptions that painters like Polygnotus created large-scale narrative paintings that were celebrated throughout Greece. Vase painting reached its artistic peak, with red-figure technique allowing painters to show fine details of anatomy, drapery, and facial expressions on pottery that served both practical and decorative purposes.

Architecture, of course, reached its culmination in the Parthenon. However, the Parthenon wasn't the only new building. The Propylaea, the monumental gateway to the Acropolis, was completed in the 430s BCE. There was the Temple of Athena Nike and the Erechtheion with its famous Porch of the Caryatids. Athens was being rebuilt as a showcase of architectural achievement. The buildings weren't just large; they were also precisely designed with subtle curves and optical refinements to appear perfectly straight and proportioned to the human eye.

The Porch of the Caryatids.[30]

All of this cultural production was interconnected with Athenian democracy and imperialism. The theater reinforced civic identity and allowed the public to explore moral questions. Philosophy questioned the very basis of society and knowledge. Sculpture and architecture made Athens physically beautiful and proclaimed its greatness to the world. Democratic participation made citizens feel invested in Athens's cultural achievements.

But this golden age was also fragile. It depended on continued peace, prosperity, and Athenian power. The empire that funded the Parthenon was creating enemies throughout Greece. The democracy that tolerated Aristophanes's mockery would eventually execute Socrates. The confidence that produced such incredible art would lead Athens into disastrous wars.

However, for a few decades in the mid-5th century BCE, everything seemed to come together in Athens. It was one of those rare historical moments when a single city produced an extraordinary concentration of talent and achievement. Playwrights, philosophers, sculptors, architects, and orators all worked in the same city at the same time, pushing each other to greater achievements and creating works that would be studied and admired for millennia.

But what was daily life actually like for ordinary Athenians living through this golden age? Behind the grand monuments and philosophical debates, people still had to eat, work, raise families, and manage households.

Most Athenians lived simply. Houses were small, built around central courtyards, with plain exteriors facing narrow streets. Wealthy homes might have multiple rooms and decorative elements, but even prosperous citizens lived modestly by modern standards. Furnishings were basic. They had beds, chairs, and storage chests. Windows were small and high up for privacy and security. The focus of the home was the hearth, sacred to the goddess Hestia, where the family cooked and gathered.

The household (*oikos*) was the fundamental unit of Athenian society. A typical household included the male head of household, his wife, children, and possibly elderly parents, along with slaves if the family could afford them, though many poorer citizens owned no slaves at all. The husband managed external affairs. The wife managed the household, supervising slaves if the family had them or doing the labor herself if not, along with organizing food production, weaving cloth, and raising young children. Respectable women rarely left the house except for religious festivals or visits to female relatives.

Food was simple but adequate. Bread was the staple, made from barley or wheat. Olives and olive oil appeared at every meal. Vegetables, such as onions, garlic, lentils, and cabbage, added variety. Fish was common; meat was expensive and usually reserved for religious festivals when sacrificed animals were cooked and shared. Wine, always diluted with water, accompanied meals. Drinking undiluted wine was considered barbaric.

The agora was the heart of daily economic and social life. Every morning, farmers brought produce to sell. Vendors offered fish, bread, pottery, cloth, tools, and everything else Athenians needed. The agora buzzed with commercial activity. Men met friends, discussed business, and heard the latest political news. It was where Socrates famously wandered, engaging passersby in philosophical conversation.

For wealthier citizens, evenings might bring symposia, which were drinking parties that were a central feature of elite male social life. These weren't wild orgies, though they could get rowdy. After dinner, men reclined on couches, drank wine, talked, sang songs, discussed philosophy, played games, and enjoyed entertainment from hired musicians or dancers. Symposia were where friendships were cemented, political alliances were formed, and ideas were exchanged among the upper classes. Women didn't attend except for hired entertainers; respectable wives stayed home.

Physical fitness was valued. Men exercised at *gymnasia*, public spaces with running tracks, wrestling grounds, and baths. Exercise wasn't just about health; it was also about cultivating the ideal body. Young men trained, older men stayed fit, and everyone socialized. The gymnasium was also an intellectual space. Philosophers taught there, conversations happened, and ideas spread.

Religious life pervaded daily existence. Household shrines honored domestic gods. Public festivals punctuated the year with processions, sacrifices, and feasts. Religion wasn't about personal salvation or moral guidance. It was more about maintaining proper relationships with the gods who could help or harm the community. Sacrifices, prayers, and rituals sought to secure divine favor and avoid divine anger.

Childhood in Athens was short. Boys from wealthy families received an education, learning to read, write, play musical instruments, and recite poetry. At age eighteen, they entered military training. Girls received no formal education, instead learning household management from their mothers. Marriage came early for girls. It is commonly believed they married at around fourteen or fifteen, though ages likely varied. Men usually married in their twenties or thirties in arrangements made by their fathers.

For all its cultural brilliance, daily life in Athens was constrained by gender, class, and status. Citizens enjoyed freedom and opportunity. Women, slaves, and metics lived more restricted lives. The golden age was golden for some (adult male citizens) and far less so for others. However, even for those who benefited, life was precarious. War, disease, and political upheaval could destroy that comfort and security in moments.

And the Peloponnesian War was coming. The long struggle between Athens and Sparta would test everything Athens had built. The golden age would not survive the war, but the cultural achievements would endure long after Athens's political power faded. The plays, the philosophy, the sculptures, and the buildings would remain, testifying to what humans could achieve when given the freedom, resources, and drive to create something that lasts.

Greek Fights Greek: The Peloponnesian War (431-404 BCE)

The war that destroyed Athens's golden age began over a minor dispute in a city most Greeks had barely heard of. However, the Peloponnesian War wasn't really about that dispute, just as World War I wasn't really about an assassination in Sarajevo. The war happened because two incompatible power structures—the Athenian naval empire and the Spartan land-based alliance—had been on a collision course for decades.

Thucydides, the Athenian general who wrote the definitive history of the war, understood this. He distinguished between the immediate causes (the specific incidents that triggered the fighting) and the real cause, which he identified as "the growth of Athenian power and the fear this caused in Sparta." Sparta watched Athens transform from an ally against Persia into an imperial power that dominated the Aegean. Spartan leaders worried that Athens's expansion would eventually threaten Sparta itself. Athens, meanwhile, believed Sparta resented Athenian success and would attack eventually anyway, so Athens might as well expand while it could.

This is a classic security dilemma. Each side's efforts to ensure its own safety made the other side feel threatened, leading to an arms race and increasing hostility until war became inevitable.

The immediate trigger came from Epidamnus and Corcyra, cities on the northwestern Greek coast. Epidamnus experienced internal conflict and asked its mother city, Corcyra, for help. Corcyra refused. Epidamnus then asked Corinth, which agreed to help. This angered Corcyra, which attacked Epidamnus. Corinth prepared a large fleet to support Epidamnus, and Corcyra, realizing it needed allies, turned to Athens.

Corcyra had a large navy, second only to Athens. If Corinth defeated Corcyra and absorbed its fleet, the balance of naval power would shift. Athens decided to ally with Corcyra, sending a small fleet to support them. A naval battle followed in 433 BCE, and Athens's presence prevented a Corinthian victory.

Corinth was furious. Corinth was a major member of Sparta's Peloponnesian League, an alliance system Sparta had built over the previous century to maintain its dominance in the Peloponnese and counter Athenian power. Unlike Athens's Delian League, which had become an empire, the Peloponnesian League gave member cities more autonomy while requiring them to follow Sparta in war. Corinthian leaders went to Sparta and demanded action against Athens, arguing that Athens's expansion threatened all of Sparta's allies and would eventually threaten Sparta itself. Other Spartan allies echoed these concerns.

Then Athens made things worse. Potidaea, a city in northern Greece, was a Corinthian colony but also a tribute-paying member of Athens's empire. Athens, worried about Potidaea's loyalty given rising tensions with Corinth, demanded that Potidaea tear down its walls, expel Corinthian magistrates, and send hostages to Athens. Potidaea refused and revolted, so Athens besieged the city. Corinth sent troops to help Potidaea. Athenian and Corinthian soldiers fought each other, though their cities weren't officially at war yet.

Finally, Athens issued the Megarian Decree, banning the city of Megara (another Spartan ally) from trading in any port controlled by Athens or its empire. This was economic warfare. Megara's economy depended on trade, and Athens controlled most major ports. The decree would strangle Megara economically.

Sparta demanded that Athens revoke the Megarian Decree and grant autonomy to its allies. Athens, led by Pericles, refused. Pericles argued that backing down would make Athens look weak and invite further demands. Better to fight now than after more concessions. Sparta's allies pressed for war. In 431 BCE, Sparta declared war on Athens, and the Peloponnesian League invaded Attica.

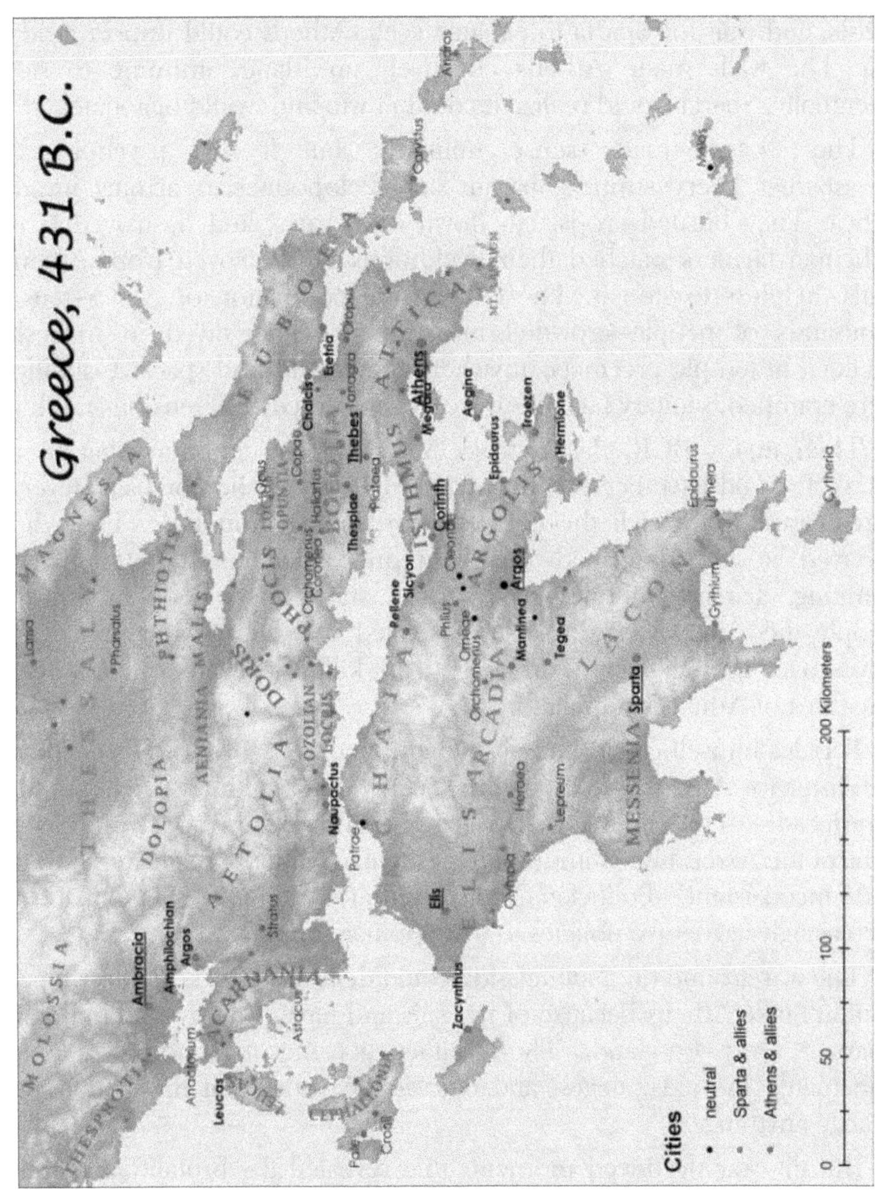

Greek cities at the beginning of the Peloponnesian War.[81]

Pericles had a strategy. Sparta's army was unbeatable on land, but Athens didn't need to fight them there. Athens had the largest navy in Greece, walls connecting the city to its port at Piraeus, and an empire that provided tribute and supplies. Pericles's plan was to avoid land battles, let the Spartans invade Attica and burn farmland if they wanted, bring the rural population inside Athens's walls, use the navy to raid Peloponnesian coasts, and wait for Sparta to exhaust itself. Athens could import food by sea. The walls made Athens effectively an island, immune to siege. Eventually, Sparta would realize it couldn't win and would negotiate.

The strategy made sense militarily, but it was psychologically devastating. Every spring, Spartan and Peloponnesian armies invaded Attica. They burned crops, cut down olive trees, and destroyed farms. Athenian farmers watched their livelihoods be destroyed from Athens's walls, helpless to stop it. The entire rural population of Attica—tens of thousands of people—crowded into Athens. They lived in makeshift shelters, in temple precincts, anywhere they could find space. Conditions were cramped, sanitary facilities were overwhelmed, and tensions ran high.

Then, in 430 BCE, plague struck Athens. We don't know what disease it was. It could have been typhus, typhoid, or a viral hemorrhagic fever. It spread rapidly through the crowded city, killing thousands. Thucydides survived it and described the symptoms: high fever, inflammation, vomiting, diarrhea, unquenchable thirst, and skin covered in pustules. People died quickly, and the bodies piled up. The plague returned in waves over the next few years, eventually killing perhaps one-quarter to one-third of Athens's population.

Pericles himself caught the plague and died in 429 BCE. His death was a disaster for Athens. He'd been the steady hand guiding Athenian policy for decades. He understood strategy, commanded respect, and could control the Assembly. Without him, Athenian leadership became unstable and inconsistent. Politicians competed for influence by proposing increasingly aggressive policies to win popular support.

The war ground on. Neither side could deliver a knockout blow. Sparta couldn't take Athens because of its walls and navy. Athens couldn't defeat Sparta's army on land. The conflict became a grinding stalemate punctuated by raids, sieges, and occasional battles that didn't decisively change anything.

But the war produced moments that revealed the brutality and moral complexity of the conflict. In 428 BCE, the city of Mytilene on the island of Lesbos revolted from Athens's empire. Athens besieged the city and forced its surrender. The question was what to do with the Mytilenians. The Athenian Assembly, angry at the betrayal, voted to execute all adult males and enslave all women and children. A ship was sent with these orders.

The next day, many Athenians felt uneasy about the decision. The Assembly met again to reconsider. Cleon, a politician who had risen to prominence after Pericles's death, argued for carrying out the execution. The Mytilenians had betrayed Athens and deserved death. Mercy would make Athens look weak and encourage other revolts. Another politician, Diodotus, argued against. Mass execution wasn't about justice; it was about whether the policy would benefit Athens. Killing everyone wouldn't stop future revolts. It would just make cities fight to the death rather than surrender. It would be better to punish the leaders and spare the people.

The Assembly reversed its decision. A second ship raced to catch the first. It arrived just in time. The massacre was called off, though the revolt's leaders were executed, and Mytilene lost its fleet and autonomy. The Mytilenian Debate, as Thucydides recorded it, showed Athenian democracy at its most volatile. It was capable of near-genocide one day and mercy the next. Decisions were driven by rhetoric and emotion rather than careful deliberation.

Two years later, in 425 BCE, Athens scored an unexpected victory. An Athenian fleet established a fort at Pylos on the Peloponnesian coast. Sparta sent forces to dislodge them, including troops stationed on the nearby island of Sphacteria. Through a combination of luck and Athenian naval skill, the Spartan forces on Sphacteria were cut off and besieged. After weeks, about 120 Spartiate hoplites, plus perioikoi and helots, surrendered.

This shocked the Greek world. Spartans didn't surrender. They fought to the death. The idea that Spartans could be trapped and forced to capitulate shattered Sparta's aura of invincibility. Athens held the prisoners as hostages, threatening to execute them if Sparta invaded Attica again. Sparta sued for peace, offering significant concessions. However, Athens, emboldened by its success and urged on by Cleon, demanded terms so harsh that Sparta refused. The war continued, but the balance of fear had shifted.

The Peace of Nicias in 421 BCE should have ended the fighting, but it created more problems than it solved. Sparta's allies felt betrayed by the terms, which favored Athens. Athens's aggressive faction wanted to continue expansion. The peace was always fragile.

In 416 BCE, Athens revealed just how ruthlessly imperial it had become. The island of Melos wanted to remain neutral in the war. Melos had historic ties to Sparta but hadn't actively helped either side. Athens demanded that Melos join its empire. The Melians argued they had the right to remain neutral. After all, they'd done nothing to harm Athens.

The discussion between Athenian envoys and Melian leaders, as Thucydides recorded it (whether historically accurate or his literary invention), became one of history's most famous statements of realpolitik. The Athenians stated bluntly, "The strong do what they can and the weak suffer what they must." Justice was irrelevant. Power determined outcomes. Melos should submit because Athens was stronger. Appeals to fairness, neutrality, or the gods were meaningless.

Melos refused to submit, so Athens besieged the island. When Melos finally surrendered, Athens executed all adult males and enslaved the women and children. The Melian massacre wasn't militarily necessary, as Melos posed no threat. It was a demonstration of power and a warning to other cities considering resistance or neutrality. Athens had become what it once fought against: an empire maintaining control through terror.

The following year would see Athens make the decision that would ultimately destroy its power. But that catastrophe was still ahead. For now, Athens seemed invincible. It was ruthless, powerful, and convinced that might made right.

Disaster in Sicily: Athens's Fatal Gamble (415–413 BCE)

In 415 BCE, the Athenian Assembly debated the most consequential decision in the city's history. The question was whether to launch a massive military expedition to conquer Sicily, a large island far to the west of Greece. It was wealthy and mostly uninvolved in the war between Athens and Sparta.

The proposal came from Alcibiades, a young, brilliant, aristocratic, and wildly ambitious man. Alcibiades was everything Athens both admired and feared: charismatic, persuasive, and brave in battle but also arrogant, self-serving, and driven more by personal glory than civic duty. He was Pericles's ward (his mother's cousin) and had learned politics from the master, but where Pericles was measured and strategic, Alcibiades was reckless and opportunistic.

Alcibiades argued that Sicily represented an incredible opportunity. The island was rich, producing grain, timber, and wealth that could fund Athens's war effort. Its major city, Syracuse, was large and powerful but politically divided. If Athens conquered Sicily, it would control the western Mediterranean, gain enormous resources, and become unstoppable. Young Athenians, tired of years of stalemate with Sparta, were seduced by dreams of easy conquest and adventure.

Nicias, the general who had negotiated the peace with Sparta, argued passionately against the expedition. He was older, more cautious, and understood how dangerous this venture was. Athens was still technically at war with Sparta, and the Peace of Nicias was collapsing. Sending Athens's best troops and ships halfway across the Mediterranean while enemies lurked at home was strategically insane. Sicily wasn't a threat to Athens. Syracuse hadn't done anything to justify an invasion. The expedition was unnecessary, expensive, and dangerous.

Nicias tried a different tactic. If the Assembly insisted on the expedition, he argued, it needed to be done properly. He listed the enormous forces that would be required: hundreds of ships, tens of thousands of soldiers, and a massive amount of supplies. He deliberately inflated the numbers, hoping to scare the Assembly into abandoning the plan. It backfired completely. The Assembly, rather than being deterred by the scale, became more excited. If the expedition needed to be that large, it must be truly important! They voted to approve everything Nicias requested and more.

In the summer of 415 BCE, Athens launched the largest military expedition in Greek history. The fleet that gathered at Piraeus numbered perhaps 134 triremes plus dozens of supply ships. It was the largest armada Athens had ever assembled. The force included over five thousand hoplites, hundreds of archers and slingers, and support personnel. Counting sailors, soldiers, and non-combatants, an estimated thirty thousand to forty thousand men were involved. The accumulated power of the empire had been poured into one massive expedition.

Three generals commanded: Alcibiades, who had pushed for the expedition; Nicias, who opposed it but was given command anyway; and Lamachus, an experienced but less politically prominent general. This divided command would prove disastrous. Alcibiades wanted aggressive action. Nicias wanted to be cautious. They couldn't agree on a strategy.

The fleet departed with a lot of fanfare and excitement. Families gathered to watch, cheering as the ships left. Athens had never seemed more powerful. The expedition felt like a celebration of Athenian greatness, a demonstration that Athens could fight Sparta and conquer Sicily at the same time. Hubris dripped from every sail.

Things started going wrong immediately. Just before departure, someone vandalized the Herms, sacred stone pillars with heads of the god Hermes. This was shocking sacrilege. Worse, rumors spread that Alcibiades and his friends were responsible for it as part of a plot against democracy. Alcibiades demanded an immediate trial to clear his name before the fleet left. His enemies refused, saying the expedition was too important to delay. Let him go, they said, and face trial when he returned.

This was a trap. After the fleet reached Sicily, Alcibiades was recalled to Athens to face charges of impiety and conspiracy. He knew what awaited him; his political enemies controlled the prosecution, and the charges carried the death penalty. Rather than return to almost certain execution, Alcibiades fled. He went to Sparta and offered his services to Athens's greatest enemy, advising the Spartans on how to defeat Athens. It was betrayal on a spectacular scale.

Herma Demosthenes.[22]

The expedition now had divided command between Nicias, who still thought the whole thing was a bad idea, and Lamachus, who wanted to attack immediately. They compromised on a cautious approach. They would sail around Sicily, gathering intelligence, trying to find allies, and delaying the actual assault on Syracuse. This gave the Syracusans time to prepare. When Athens finally laid siege to Syracuse, the city was ready.

The siege of Syracuse became a grinding stalemate. Athens built walls around the city to cut it off. Syracuse built counter-walls. Battles were fought. Ground was gained and lost. Lamachus was killed in battle, leaving only Nicias in command. Syracuse received reinforcements from other Sicilian cities and, critically, from Sparta. A Spartan general named Gylippus arrived with troops and took command of Syracuse's defense. He was competent, aggressive, and understood Athenian tactics. The balance shifted.

Athens sent another massive fleet with thousands more soldiers under the general Demosthenes. For a moment, it seemed Athens might still win through sheer weight of numbers. However, the reinforcements couldn't break the deadlock either. The siege dragged into its second year. Athenian soldiers were dying from disease, exhaustion, and combat. Supplies ran low, and morale collapsed.

By 413 BCE, even Nicias recognized the expedition had failed. The generals decided to retreat. It would be a humiliating defeat, but at least the army and fleet would survive to fight another day. But then there was a lunar eclipse. The Athenian soothsayers interpreted this as a bad omen and warned against immediate departure. Nicias, who was deeply religious and superstitious, delayed the retreat for nearly a month to wait for better omens.

That delay was catastrophic. The Syracusans realized the Athenians were planning to escape and moved to prevent it. They attacked the Athenian fleet in Syracuse's harbor. The battle was desperate and chaotic. Ships rammed each other in confined waters, marines fought on decks, and the harbor became choked with wreckage. The Athenian fleet was destroyed. Most of the ships were sunk or captured. Thousands of sailors drowned.

With the fleet gone, the Athenian army was trapped. They tried to retreat overland, marching through Sicily while Syracusan forces constantly harassed them. The retreat became a nightmare. Soldiers died from thirst, exhaustion, and attacks. The army fragmented. Nicias and Demosthenes tried to maintain order, but discipline broke down.

Finally, the Syracusans caught up with the retreating army and surrounded them. The Athenians surrendered. Nicias and Demosthenes were executed despite promises of mercy. The captured soldiers were imprisoned in stone quarries outside Syracuse. The quarries were open to the sun and rain, with no shelter, little food, and less water. Men died by the hundreds from exposure, disease, and starvation. Some were eventually sold as slaves. Most died in the quarries.

Of the massive force Athens sent to Sicily—perhaps forty thousand men total, including reinforcements—only a handful of the captured soldiers ever returned home. Nearly two hundred ships were lost. Thousands of Athens's best soldiers, sailors, and officers were dead or enslaved. It was the worst military disaster Athens ever experienced, and it was one of the worst disasters in all of Greek military history.

The psychological impact was as devastating as the material loss. Athens had seemed invincible. The expedition to Sicily was supposed to prove Athenian greatness. Instead, it demonstrated Athenian hubris, poor leadership, and the limits of Athenian power. The disaster showed every subject city that Athens could be beaten.

The End: Athens's Final Struggle and Surrender (413–404 BCE)

After the Sicilian disaster, most observers expected Athens to surrender within months. The city had lost a devastating number of its military-age male citizens, most of its fleet, and its treasury was nearly empty. Subject cities across the empire saw weakness and revolted. Persia, recognizing an opportunity to weaken Greece and reclaim the Ionian cities, began funding Sparta to build a fleet capable of challenging Athens at sea.

But Athens refused to quit. The city's resilience was extraordinary. Using reserve funds stored on the Acropolis (silver that had been set aside for absolute emergencies), Athens built a new fleet. Democratic institutions continued functioning. The Assembly still met, and citizens still served on juries. Athens maintained control over enough of its empire to collect some tribute. The war continued.

Sparta changed its strategy on the advice of the traitor Alcibiades (who later fled Sparta for Persia after allegedly seducing a Spartan queen). Instead of seasonal invasions, Sparta established a permanent fort at Decelea in northern Attica. This was far more damaging than previous raids. Athenian farmers couldn't work their land. Over twenty thousand slaves fled to the Spartans, including skilled workers from the silver mines at Laurium. Athens's silver production collapsed. The city was under constant pressure and harassment, even though its walls still protected it.

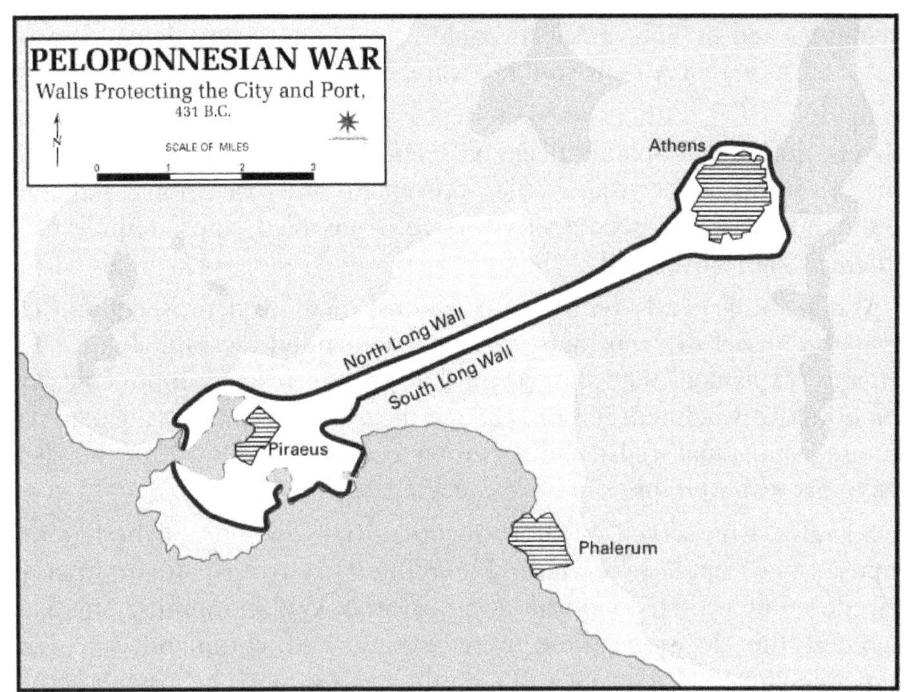

The walls protecting Athens during the war.[38]

Athens also tore itself apart politically. In 411 BCE, a group of oligarchs staged a coup, overthrowing democracy and establishing the rule of the Four Hundred. The oligarchs argued that Persia would only support Athens if it abandoned democracy for oligarchy. The coup was supposed to end the war on favorable terms. Instead, it divided Athens. The Athenian fleet stationed at Samos refused to recognize the oligarchy and remained democratic. The Four Hundred quickly collapsed, replaced by the more moderate regime of the Five Thousand, which eventually restored full democracy. The internal turmoil wasted energy Athens couldn't afford to lose.

The war's final phase was a series of naval battles for control of the Hellespont, the narrow strait connecting the Aegean to the Black Sea. Athens depended on grain imported from the Black Sea region. Without access to the Hellespont, Athens would starve. Sparta, with Persian gold building fleet after fleet, could finally challenge Athens at sea.

Athens won several impressive naval victories in these years. Athenian sailors and admirals proved that even after Sicily, they were superb. However, the strategic equation had changed fundamentally. Athens couldn't afford to lose ships because it couldn't afford to replace them.

Sparta, backed by Persian silver, could rebuild after every defeat. It was a war of attrition that Athens couldn't win.

In 406 BCE, Athens won a major naval victory at the Arginusae Islands, defeating a Spartan fleet and securing the Hellespont temporarily. But a storm after the battle prevented the victorious Athenian commanders from rescuing survivors from disabled ships. Hundreds of Athenian sailors drowned.

When the generals returned to Athens, they faced prosecution. The Assembly, grief-stricken and furious, demanded accountability. The generals explained that the storm had made rescue impossible, but emotion overwhelmed reason. In an illegal single vote (Athenian law required individual trials), the Assembly condemned all eight generals to death. Six who were present were executed.

Socrates, who served in the council that day, was one of the few who opposed the illegal procedure. He refused to participate in what he considered unjust. His opposition was ignored. Within months, Athenians regretted the decision; these were experienced commanders Athens desperately needed. However, the damage was done. The Arginusae trial showed democracy at its worst: emotion overruling law, grief producing injustice, and the mob condemning the men who had just saved them.

In 405 BCE, the war ended at Aegospotami on the Hellespont. The Athenian fleet, numbering about 180 ships, was beached. The Spartan admiral Lysander surprised them at dawn before most crews had even boarded their vessels. It was slaughter, not battle. The Spartans captured or destroyed almost the entire Athenian fleet. Thousands of captured Athenian sailors were reportedly executed. Athens's navy, the source of its power for seventy years, was obliterated in a single morning.

Without ships, Athens couldn't import food. Sparta besieged Athens by land and blockaded Piraeus by sea. Through the winter of 405/404 BCE, Athens starved. Food supplies dwindled and then disappeared. People died in the streets. Desperate Athenians debated what to do. Some wanted to fight to the death. Others argued for surrender. The Assembly, starving and desperate, finally voted to negotiate.

The terms demanded by Sparta were harsh. Athens would lose its entire empire. Every subject city would be freed from Athenian control. The Long Walls connecting Athens to Piraeus would be torn down, leaving Athens defenseless. All remaining ships except twelve patrol vessels would be surrendered. Athens would become Sparta's ally, following Spartan foreign policy. Democracy would be abolished and replaced with an oligarchy.

Some of Sparta's allies, particularly Corinth and Thebes, demanded harsher terms. They wanted Athens destroyed completely. Sparta refused. The Spartans reportedly said that Athens had saved Greece from Persia, and for that service, Athens deserved to survive. Whether this was genuine gratitude or cold strategic calculation (destroying Athens would make Sparta's allies too powerful), Sparta insisted on terms that preserved Athens as a city, if not as a power.

In spring 404 BCE, Athens surrendered. The walls came down to the sound of flutes. Spartans and their allies celebrated as the fortifications that had made Athens invincible were demolished stone by stone. The remaining ships were handed over. Democracy was abolished. An oligarchy of thirty pro-Spartan Athenians, known as the Thirty Tyrants, took power and ruled through terror, executing or exiling democratic leaders and confiscating property. The Thirty Tyrants' reign lasted eight brutal months before democratic forces overthrew them and restored democracy in 403 BCE.

The Peloponnesian War had lasted twenty-seven years (431–404 BCE, interrupted by the six-year Peace of Nicias). It killed tens of thousands of Greeks, destroyed cities, impoverished regions, and weakened the Greek world. Athens lost everything: its empire, its fleet, its wealth, its power, and its confidence.

Thucydides wrote his history of the Peloponnesian War believing it would be "a possession for all time." It was not just a chronicle of events but a study of human nature, power, and the dynamics of conflict. He was right. The Peloponnesian War demonstrated how fear and ambition drive states into war, how confidence leads to overreach, how democracies can make catastrophic decisions through emotion, and how wars consume everything and last far longer than anyone expects.

The golden age of Athens died with the war. The Parthenon still stood. The plays were still performed. Philosophical inquiry continued. But the confidence, the wealth, and the sense that Athens was destined for greatness were gone. Greece would never again reach the heights it had achieved in 5th-century Athens. The brief moment when a single city combined democracy, imperial power, and cultural brilliance had ended, and it would not come again.

Sparta won the war but proved incapable of managing peace. Sparta's dominance lasted barely thirty years. The Spartans proved as oppressive as Athens had been, installing oligarchies in cities that had hoped for freedom and acting as Greece's new imperial power. Sparta's arrogance and brutality turned former allies into enemies. In 371 BCE, the Theban general Epaminondas shattered Spartan military supremacy at the Battle of Leuctra. Using revolutionary tactics (massing troops in an unprecedented deep formation on one wing), Epaminondas defeated the supposedly invincible Spartan army and killed one of Sparta's two kings. For the first time in two centuries, Sparta had been decisively beaten in open battle.

Thebes became Greece's dominant power, but its supremacy was brief. Epaminondas invaded the Peloponnese, liberated Messenia from Spartan control (freeing the helots who had been enslaved for centuries), and reduced Sparta to a second-rate power. But when Epaminondas died in battle at Mantinea in 362 BCE, Theban power collapsed with him. Greece descended into a chaotic free-for-all with no dominant power. Exhausted city-states constantly fought each other, and there was no end in sight. This was the weakened, divided Greek world that Macedon would conquer a generation later.

Chapter 7 – The Hellenistic Sweep: From Macedonia to World Empire

The Rough North: The Rise of Macedon

For centuries, the Greek city-states barely noticed Macedonia. The kingdom to the north was perceived as a backwater by southern Greeks. It was rural, mountainous, politically unstable, and culturally different in ways that southern Greeks often dismissed as backward. Macedonians spoke a Greek dialect that city Greeks could barely understand. They were ruled by kings rather than assemblies, lived in scattered villages rather than urban centers, and maintained a warrior aristocracy that seemed more barbarian than Hellenic to sophisticated urbanites. Many Athenians and Spartans viewed Macedonians as crude rustics, often dismissing them as barely Greek at all.

This condescension was a fatal mistake. In the mid-4th century BCE, Macedonia would conquer all of Greece, and a Macedonian king would build an empire stretching from Greece to India. The city-states that had dominated Greek politics for centuries would become subjects of a northern kingdom they had dismissed as irrelevant.

The transformation began with Philip II, who became king of Macedonia in 359 BCE. Philip inherited a kingdom in crisis. His predecessor had been killed in battle against the Illyrians. The royal treasury was empty. Multiple pretenders claimed the throne. Macedonia's neighbors, namely the Illyrians, Paeonians, and Thracians, all saw an opportunity to raid or conquer Macedonian territory. The kingdom seemed likely to fragment or be absorbed by its enemies.

Philip was twenty-three years old, but he'd spent three years as a hostage in Thebes during the city's brief period of dominance in the 360s BCE. Scholars generally hypothesize that during his time in Thebes, Philip observed the military innovations of Epaminondas, the general who had broken Spartan power at the Battle of Leuctra in 371 BCE. Epaminondas had revolutionized Greek warfare by massing troops in deep formations and using coordinated movements rather than simple frontal charges. Philip is thought to have learned these lessons well, though ancient sources don't explicitly confirm this connection.

Philip's first priority was survival. He bought off some enemies with tribute, made alliances with others, and dealt with the most immediate threats through quick, decisive campaigns. Within two years, he'd secured Macedonia's borders and eliminated rival claimants to the throne. Then he began building.

Philip transformed the Macedonian army into the most formidable fighting force in the Greek world. His innovations combined Greek military tactics with Macedonian advantages in cavalry and manpower. The result was an army that proved capable of defeating any Greek city-state and most combinations of city-states in the battles it fought.

The centerpiece of Philip's military revolution was the *sarissa*, a pike between thirteen and twenty-one feet long, roughly twice the length of a standard Greek spear. Macedonian infantry, organized in a phalanx, wielded these enormous pikes with both hands. The front five ranks could all project their sarissas forward, creating a nearly impenetrable forest of spearheads. Enemy hoplites with their shorter spears couldn't reach Macedonian soldiers without first breaking through multiple ranks of pikes.

Macedonian phalanx.[24]

The Macedonian phalanx was devastating but inflexible. It could move forward in formation but struggled with rough terrain, turning, or responding to threats from the flanks or rear. Philip solved this problem by combining the phalanx with elite infantry called *hypaspists*, who fought with shorter weapons and could maneuver more flexibly and, most importantly, with heavy cavalry.

Macedonian cavalry, drawn from the kingdom's aristocracy, was far superior to cavalry in southern Greece. The Macedonian Companions rode larger horses, wielded long lances, and trained constantly for coordinated charges. They were shock troops who could smash through enemy formations or exploit gaps created by the phalanx. Philip used cavalry and infantry together in combined-arms tactics that no Greek city-state could match.

Philip also professionalized his army in ways Greek city-states never had. Macedonian soldiers were paid, trained year-round, and served on long campaigns far from home. Greek city-states relied on citizen-soldiers who served for limited periods and wanted to return to their farms. Philip's professionals could campaign continuously, besiege cities for months, and march hundreds of miles. They were a standing army, not a militia.

With this military machine, Philip began expanding. He didn't immediately attack the major Greek city-states. Instead, he moved methodically through the north, conquering Thrace and gaining control of gold and silver mines, which made Macedonia wealthy. He established or captured cities along the coast, building a fleet and securing trade routes. He intervened in regional conflicts to expand Macedonian influence.

Southern Greeks initially ignored Philip's expansion. They were absorbed in their own conflicts. Thebes and Sparta had exhausted each other. Athens had partially recovered from the Peloponnesian War but was primarily interested in rebuilding its naval power and protecting trade routes, not fighting land wars in the north. The Greek cities saw Philip as a local power, maybe a nuisance, but not a threat to them.

The Athenian orator Demosthenes saw things differently. From the 350s BCE onward, Demosthenes delivered speech after speech warning Athens that Philip was dangerous, that every Macedonian expansion brought Philip closer to controlling all Greece, and that Athens needed to act before it was too late. These speeches, called the Philippics, are masterpieces of rhetoric. They're also case studies in how democracies struggle to respond to distant threats until it's too late.

Demosthenes faced several problems. First, Philip was clever about not provoking Athens directly. He expanded into regions Athens didn't care much about. Philip actually sent diplomatic letters expressing friendship and avoided open conflict with major city-states. Second, Athenians were war-weary and focused on commerce, not military adventures. Third, Philip had allies in Athens, politicians who argued he was reasonable, that accommodation was possible, and that Demosthenes was a warmonger exaggerating the threat.

By the time Athens recognized the danger, Philip controlled most of northern Greece and was moving south. In 346 BCE, Athens made peace with Philip, essentially conceding his conquests in exchange for promises to respect southern Greek independence. Philip used the peace to consolidate his gains and prepare for the next phase.

The final confrontation came in 338 BCE. Philip intervened in a conflict called the Sacred War, positioning himself as a defender of Greek religious sites. Athens and Thebes, finally recognizing that Philip intended to dominate all Greece, formed an alliance to stop him. The two sides met at Chaeronea in central Greece.

The combined Athenian-Theban army outnumbered Philip's forces, and they were fighting on familiar terrain. However, Philip's army was professional, trained, and led by the best general of the age. Philip used his cavalry, commanded by his eighteen-year-old son Alexander, to devastating effect. The Macedonian phalanx broke the Athenian and Theban lines. Thebes's elite Sacred Band—three hundred warriors who'd never been defeated—were destroyed, fighting to the death rather than surrender according to ancient sources, though whether literally every man fell or a handful survived remains uncertain.

Athens and Thebes were defeated. Philip could have destroyed both cities, but he chose a different approach. He made moderate peace terms with Athens. There would be no destruction or occupation, but Athens had to acknowledge Macedonian supremacy. Thebes was treated more harshly, but it was not destroyed either. Philip understood that destroying famous Greek cities would create resentment.

Philip then organized the Greek city-states into the League of Corinth in 337 BCE. Every major Greek city except Sparta joined. The league supposedly guaranteed Greek autonomy and peace, but Philip was elected *hegemon*, or military leader. Macedonia controlled Greek foreign policy. The city-states were autonomous in theory but subjects in practice.

Philip announced that the League of Corinth would invade Persia to avenge the Persian invasions of 490 and 480 BCE. This was brilliant propaganda. Philip cast himself as the champion of Greek civilization, leading a panhellenic crusade against the barbarians who'd once threatened Greece. It united Greeks behind a common cause (or at least gave them a common enemy), and it promised glory and wealth from conquering the richest empire in the world.

However, Philip never led the invasion. In 336 BCE, at his daughter's wedding, Philip was assassinated by one of his bodyguards. The motives remain unclear. It could have been a personal grudge, a political conspiracy, or both. Philip was forty-six years old. He'd transformed Macedonia from an obscure kingdom into the dominant power in Greece in just twenty-three years.

His son, Alexander, was twenty years old. He had been trained by the best general in the world and educated by Aristotle. Alexander would take his father's army and plans and do something even Philip probably hadn't imagined: conquer the Persian Empire and change the ancient world forever.

The rise of Macedonia under Philip marked the end of the classical Greek world of independent city-states. The politically independent, polis-centered civilization that had produced Athens's democracy, Sparta's military excellence, and the cultural achievements of the 5th and 4th centuries was finished. The future belonged to kingdoms and empires, not citizen assemblies. Greek culture would spread across the Mediterranean and into Asia, but it would do so as the culture of conquerors and colonizers, not as the achievement of autonomous city-states.

A World at His Feet: The Conquests of Alexander the Great

Alexander became king of Macedonia in 336 BCE at the age of twenty, inheriting his father's kingdom, army, and plan to invade Persia. What he did with that inheritance would make him the most famous conqueror in ancient history and fundamentally reshape the Mediterranean and Near Eastern world.

Alexander's education had prepared him for greatness, or at least convinced him he was destined for it. Philip had hired Aristotle, the greatest philosopher of the age, to tutor Alexander and a group of young Macedonian nobles. For three years, Aristotle taught Alexander literature, philosophy, science, and ethics. Alexander developed a lifelong love of Homer's *Iliad*, reportedly sleeping with a copy of it under his pillow and seeing himself as a new Achilles. Whether Aristotle's philosophical teachings deeply influenced Alexander's worldview is debated, but the connection between the greatest conqueror and the greatest philosopher became legendary.

Alexander's military education came from his father and from experience. He commanded cavalry units at Chaeronea at age eighteen, proving himself brave and capable. He learned strategy from watching Philip, absorbed the mechanics of siege warfare, and understood combined-arms tactics. When his father was assassinated, Alexander was ready. He was militarily competent, intellectually confident, and burning with ambition.

However, Alexander's succession wasn't automatic. He was young and untested as king. Some Macedonian nobles supported rival claimants. Greek city-states, seeing an opportunity in the chaos following Philip's death, began discussing revolt. Thebes actually did revolt, expecting other cities to join and thinking the young king couldn't control his kingdom and fight Greece at the same time.

Alexander moved with devastating speed. He marched south to Thebes with his army. When Thebes refused to surrender, he destroyed the city. Thebes was razed. Its population was largely enslaved, and others were killed. Only the house of the poet Pindar and the temples were spared. The message was clear: revolt against Alexander meant annihilation. The other Greek cities quickly reaffirmed their membership in the League of Corinth. No one else tried to rebel.

With Greece secured, Alexander turned to Persia. In the spring of 334 BCE, he crossed the Hellespont into Asia Minor with an army of perhaps forty thousand to fifty thousand men–Macedonians, Greeks from the League of Corinth, and various allies. It was a large force by Greek standards, but it was tiny compared to the resources the Persian Empire could mobilize. Persia controlled territory from Egypt to India, commanded millions of subjects, and possessed wealth that dwarfed anything Greece could imagine.

Alexander's invasion was audacious to the point of madness. He was attacking the largest empire in the world with an army that, if destroyed, couldn't be replaced. He had no fleet to speak of, while Persia controlled the seas. He was heading into hostile territory thousands of miles from home, where Persian armies could attack from multiple directions. A sensible strategic analysis suggested that Alexander would be defeated, probably quickly.

Alexander won his first major battle at the Granicus River in May 334 BCE, just days after crossing into Asia. Persian satraps had gathered an army to stop the invasion. They chose to fight at the Granicus, a river with steep banks that would force Alexander's army to fight at a disadvantage while crossing. It was a reasonable defensive plan.

Alexander attacked anyway, personally leading the cavalry charge into the river and up the opposite bank while under fire. It was reckless and nearly got him killed. His helmet was split by a sword blow, and one of his Companions saved his life. But the charge succeeded. The Macedonian cavalry broke the Persian line, the phalanx followed, and the Persian army collapsed. The satraps fled or died. The psychological impact was enormous. The Persians weren't invincible.

Alexander spent the next year conquering western Asia Minor. Cities opened their gates, sometimes welcoming him as a liberator from Persian rule. He "freed" Greek cities from Persian control, though in practice, they became subject to Macedonia. He captured coastal cities that could serve as bases for the Persian fleet, gradually neutralizing Persia's naval advantage by controlling the ports.

The Persian king, Darius III, wasn't taking Alexander seriously enough. Darius assumed Alexander was a minor problem that the satraps could handle. When those satraps kept losing, Darius finally assembled a royal army and marched to confront Alexander personally in 333 BCE. The two armies met at Issus, on the coast of what is now southern Turkey.

Darius had more soldiers. Ancient sources claim he had hundreds of thousands, though modern estimates suggest perhaps 80,000 to 100,000. Alexander had perhaps forty thousand men. However, Darius made a crucial mistake. He chose to fight on narrow coastal ground where he couldn't use his numerical superiority effectively. Numbers mattered less when armies couldn't deploy in broad formations.

Alexander deployed his phalanx in the center, cavalry on the wings, and waited for Darius to attack. When Persian forces engaged the phalanx, Alexander led a cavalry charge aimed directly at Darius's position. This was Alexander's signature tactic: use the phalanx to fix the enemy in place, then smash through with heavy cavalry aimed at the enemy commander. It worked brilliantly. Alexander's Companions broke through the Persian lines and drove toward Darius himself.

Darius panicked and fled. Once the king ran, the Persian army's morale collapsed. The battle became a rout. Thousands of Persians were killed in the retreat. Alexander captured Darius's camp, including his mother, wife, and children. Darius escaped, but his prestige was in tatters. The Persian king had run from battle. Alexander treated the royal family with respect and sent messages to Darius offering peace in exchange for half the Persian Empire.

Darius refused. He was still king of Persia, and he thought he could defeat this Macedonian upstart. Alexander, for his part, wasn't interested in half of Persia. He wanted it all.

Alexander spent the next two years conquering the eastern Mediterranean coast. He besieged Tyre for seven months, eventually building a causeway to the island city and taking it by storm. He conquered Gaza after another difficult siege. He entered Egypt, where he was welcomed as a liberator from Persian rule and crowned pharaoh. While in Egypt, he visited the oracle of Amun at the Siwa Oasis. What the oracle told him is unknown, but Alexander emerged claiming divine parentage. He was the son of Zeus-Amun. Whether he believed this or used it for propaganda, it reinforced his growing sense of destiny.

By 331 BCE, Alexander controlled the entire eastern Mediterranean coast. He'd cut off Persia from the sea, secured his supply lines, and prepared for the final confrontation with Darius. He marched into Mesopotamia, seeking battle. Darius assembled another massive army and chose the battlefield carefully. This time, they would fight on the plains near Gaugamela, where flat, open ground would let him use his numerical advantage and cavalry effectively.

The Battle of Gaugamela in October 331 BCE was the decisive engagement of the war. Darius commanded perhaps 100,000 to 250,000 troops (the numbers are disputed and probably exaggerated by ancient sources, but he significantly outnumbered Alexander). His army included cavalry from across the empire, Greek mercenaries, and scythed chariots designed to break formations. It was the largest army Persia could field, and Darius was personally commanding it.

Alexander had perhaps forty-seven thousand troops. He was outnumbered roughly two-to-one at the minimum, possibly more. Darius's plan was to use his cavalry superiority to envelop Alexander's flanks while the center held. The scythed chariots would disrupt the Macedonian phalanx.

Alexander's response showed his tactical genius. He deployed his phalanx in the center with gaps that allowed the chariots to pass through harmlessly, allowing the light troops to kill the chariot crews. He strengthened his flanks to prevent envelopment. Then he personally led a cavalry charge aimed at a weak point in the Persian line, not straight at Darius this time, but at an angle, targeting the junction between the Persian cavalry and infantry.

The charge broke through. Alexander's Companions drove deep into the Persian formation, wheeling toward Darius's position. Once again, Darius fled. And once again, his army's morale collapsed when the king ran. The battle became a massacre. Thousands of Persians died in the retreat. Alexander pursued, but he couldn't catch Darius.

Gaugamela destroyed the Persian Empire's ability to resist. Darius still lived and still claimed to be king, but his armies were broken. Alexander marched into Persia's heartland unopposed. Babylon opened its gates in welcome. Susa surrendered. Alexander entered Persepolis, the ceremonial capital of Persia, in January 330 BCE.

What happened next is controversial. According to ancient sources, during a drinking party, Alexander and his companions set fire to the royal palace complex at Persepolis. Whether this was deliberate revenge for Xerxes burning Athens 150 years earlier, drunken vandalism, or a symbolic statement that Persian power was finished, the result was the same: the center of Persian royalty went up in flames.

Alexander pursued Darius eastward. In July 330 BCE, Darius's own satraps, recognizing the war was lost and hoping to curry favor with Alexander, murdered Darius and fled. Alexander found Darius's body and gave him a royal funeral. The Persian Empire, which had dominated the Near East for over two centuries, no longer existed. Alexander was now king of Asia.

Mosaic of Alexander fighting Darius III.[25]

Most conquerors would have stopped. Alexander had achieved something unprecedented. A Macedonian king controlled one of the largest empires the world had ever seen. He could consolidate his gains, organize his conquests, and return home in triumph. Instead, Alexander kept going.

He spent the next three years (330–327 BCE) conquering central Asia. This was a brutal, grinding campaign. The satraps who'd killed Darius led a resistance. Local populations rebelled. The terrain was harsh, full of mountains, deserts, and hostile territory. Alexander's army besieged fortresses, fought guerrillas, and endured hardships far from home. The men wanted to go back to Macedonia. Alexander insisted on pushing forward, conquering every region that had once been part of the Persian Empire.

During this period, Alexander's character darkened. Power and constant victory were changing him. He adopted Persian royal customs, wearing Persian dress and attempting to require *proskynesis* (prostration before the king), a custom he tried to impose on his Macedonian and Greek companions with little success, as they found it deeply offensive. Greeks didn't prostrate themselves before anyone. Alexander executed Philotas, one of his commanders, on charges of conspiracy, and killed Philotas's father, Parmenion, one of Philip's most trusted generals. In a drunken rage at Samarkand in 328 BCE, Alexander personally killed Cleitus, one of his oldest companions, who'd saved his life at the Granicus. Cleitus had criticized Alexander for adopting Persian customs and claiming divine parentage.

Alexander regretted killing Cleitus, but the incident showed how paranoid and autocratic he had become. The young king who'd studied philosophy with Aristotle was becoming increasingly autocratic and tolerated no dissent. The army obeyed out of fear and discipline rather than love.

In 327 BCE, Alexander invaded India. He crossed the Hindu Kush mountains and entered the Punjab region, winning a major battle against King Porus at the Hydaspes River in 326 BCE. Porus commanded war elephants, animals the Macedonians had never fought before. Alexander won anyway, using cavalry to attack the elephants from the flanks and drive them back into Porus's own infantry.

Alexander's army had reached its limit. The soldiers had been campaigning continuously for eight years. They'd marched thousands of miles from home through deserts, mountains, and jungles. They'd fought dozens of battles. They'd seen companions die far from home. Rumors said Alexander wanted to continue east, conquering more of India, perhaps reaching the edge of the world. The army mutinied, not violently, but they refused to go farther.

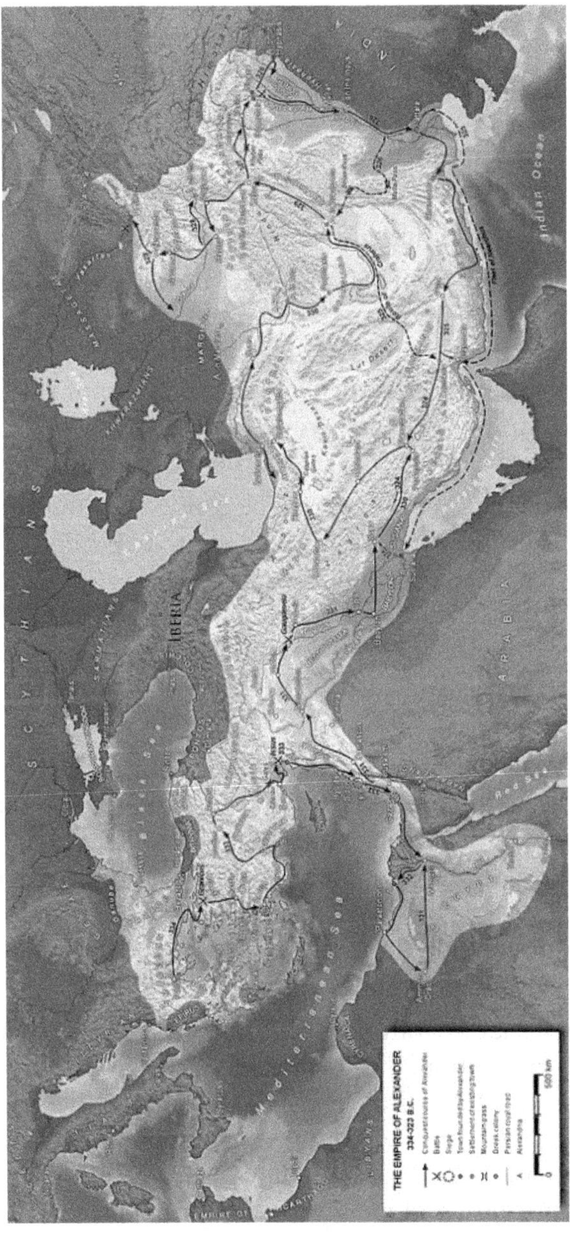

Alexander's empire at its greatest extent.[26]

Alexander tried persuasion, threats, and sulking. None of it worked. The army wouldn't move. Finally, Alexander had to accept reality. He ordered a return, but rather than retracing his route, he marched his army through the Gedrosian Desert in southern Iran—one of the most hostile environments on Earth. It was an extremely costly ordeal that killed thousands of soldiers and support personnel from thirst, heat, and starvation.

Alexander reached Babylon in 323 BCE and began planning new campaigns. He never stopped thinking about conquest. However, in June 323 BCE, after a night of heavy drinking, Alexander fell ill. Over ten days, he grew progressively weaker. On June 10th or 11th, 323 BCE, Alexander died in Babylon. He was thirty-two years old.

The cause of death remains debated. It could have been fever from disease (malaria, typhoid, or something else), complications from wounds and years of hard living, or poison. The ancient sources can't agree. What is clear is that Alexander's death created an immediate crisis. He'd conquered an empire stretching from Greece to India, but he made no provisions for succession.

Alexander's achievements were staggering. In thirteen years, he'd conquered the Persian Empire, invaded central Asia and India, founded over twenty cities (many named Alexandria), and spread Greek culture across the Near East. He'd never lost a pitched battle. He'd personally led cavalry charges in nearly every major engagement. He was brave to the point of recklessness, brilliant tactically, and driven by ambition that bordered on madness.

Alexander the Great was a conqueror, not an administrator. The empire he built was held together by his charisma and military force, not by institutions or sustainable governance. His treatment of conquered peoples varied wildly; he could be generous or brutal. He promoted cultural fusion, marrying a Persian princess and encouraging his men to marry local women, but this was as much about binding the empire together as about genuine cultural appreciation.

Alexander's legacy is complex. He destroyed the Persian Empire and ended Persian domination of the Near East. He spread Greek culture and language across vast territories, creating the Hellenistic world that would last for centuries. He inspired countless later conquerors who saw him as the ultimate warrior-king. However, he also left a trail of destroyed cities, massacred populations, and an empire that immediately fell apart after his death because it depended entirely on him.

The Splintered Kingdom: The Wars of the Diadochi

When Alexander died in June 323 BCE, he left behind an empire stretching from Greece to India and a question that would kill thousands: who would inherit everything?

Alexander's deathbed succession was a disaster. His half-brother Arrhidaeus was mentally disabled and couldn't rule. His wife, Roxana, was pregnant but hadn't given birth yet. According to legend, Alexander's generals gathered around him as he lay dying and asked who should inherit the empire. Alexander supposedly whispered "the strongest," though he may have been trying to say "Krateros," the name of one of his generals. Or maybe he was too weak to speak at all, and someone made up the answer later. Either way, the ambiguity guaranteed civil war.

The generals, known as the Diadochi, or "successors," tried to keep up appearances at first. They declared Arrhidaeus king (renaming him Philip III) and agreed that if Roxana's baby was a boy, he'd be co-king. Roxana did have a son, named Alexander IV. So, the empire officially had two kings: one who was too mentally incompetent to rule and one who couldn't walk yet. The real power belonged to the generals who commanded armies.

They divided the empire like mob bosses carving up territory. Perdiccas, who'd been Alexander's second-in-command, became regent. Ptolemy grabbed Egypt and never let go. Antigonus took much of Asia Minor. Lysimachus got Thrace. Seleucus received Babylonia. Antipater, who had been running Macedonia while Alexander conquered Asia, kept Greece and Macedonia.

This arrangement lasted about two years before everyone started killing each other.

These weren't bureaucrats content with safe administrative posts. They were conquerors who'd followed Alexander across the known world. They had led cavalry charges, besieged cities, and defeated armies. They were ambitious, ruthless, and commanded soldiers who'd follow them anywhere. Asking them to peacefully share power was like asking wolves to share a kill.

The Wars of the Diadochi spanned roughly forty years, with the decisive phase ending around 281 BCE. The fighting was spectacularly brutal. Alliances formed and dissolved overnight. Former friends betrayed each other. Armies marched thousands of miles to fight battles that changed nothing. Both of Alexander's heirs were murdered: Philip III in

317 BCE, young Alexander IV and his mother Roxana in 310 BCE. With the legitimate heirs dead, the pretense evaporated. The Diadochi stopped claiming to rule for Alexander's family and started building their own kingdoms.

Perdiccas, the regent who tried to hold everything together, made himself everyone's enemy and was murdered by his own officers in 321 BCE while invading Egypt. Eumenes, probably the most talented general of the bunch but handicapped by not being Macedonian, fought brilliantly for years trying to preserve Alexander's empire. He was eventually betrayed by his own troops and executed in 316 BCE. Craterus, one of Alexander's most respected generals, died in battle in 321 BCE. The list of the dead grew longer every year.

The survivor who scared everyone was Antigonus One-Eye (yes, that was actually what they called him). By the 310s BCE, Antigonus controlled most of Asia Minor and parts of Syria. He had the resources and ambition to reunite Alexander's empire under his own rule. This terrified the other Diadochi, who hated each other but feared Antigonus more. They formed a coalition against him.

The final showdown came at Ipsus in 301 BCE. Antigonus was eighty years old—ancient by Greek standards—and, according to estimates, commanded around seventy thousand troops. Against him stood a coalition led by Seleucus and Lysimachus with comparable numbers, supplemented by 480 war elephants reportedly provided by the Indian king Chandragupta Maurya in exchange for territory. The elephants would prove decisive.

Antigonus's son Demetrius, who'd later earn the nickname "Besieger of Cities," led a devastating cavalry charge that broke through the coalition's lines. It was a brilliant move that should have won the battle. However, Seleucus used his elephants to cut off Demetrius's return. The elephants formed a living wall that the cavalry couldn't penetrate. Antigonus, abandoned by his cavalry, watched his infantry collapse. He died fighting, defiant to the end. His death ended any hope of reuniting Alexander's empire.

After Ipsus, the empire was permanently fractured and effectively divided into separate kingdoms. The political map crystallized around three major kingdoms that would dominate the Greek world for the next two centuries.

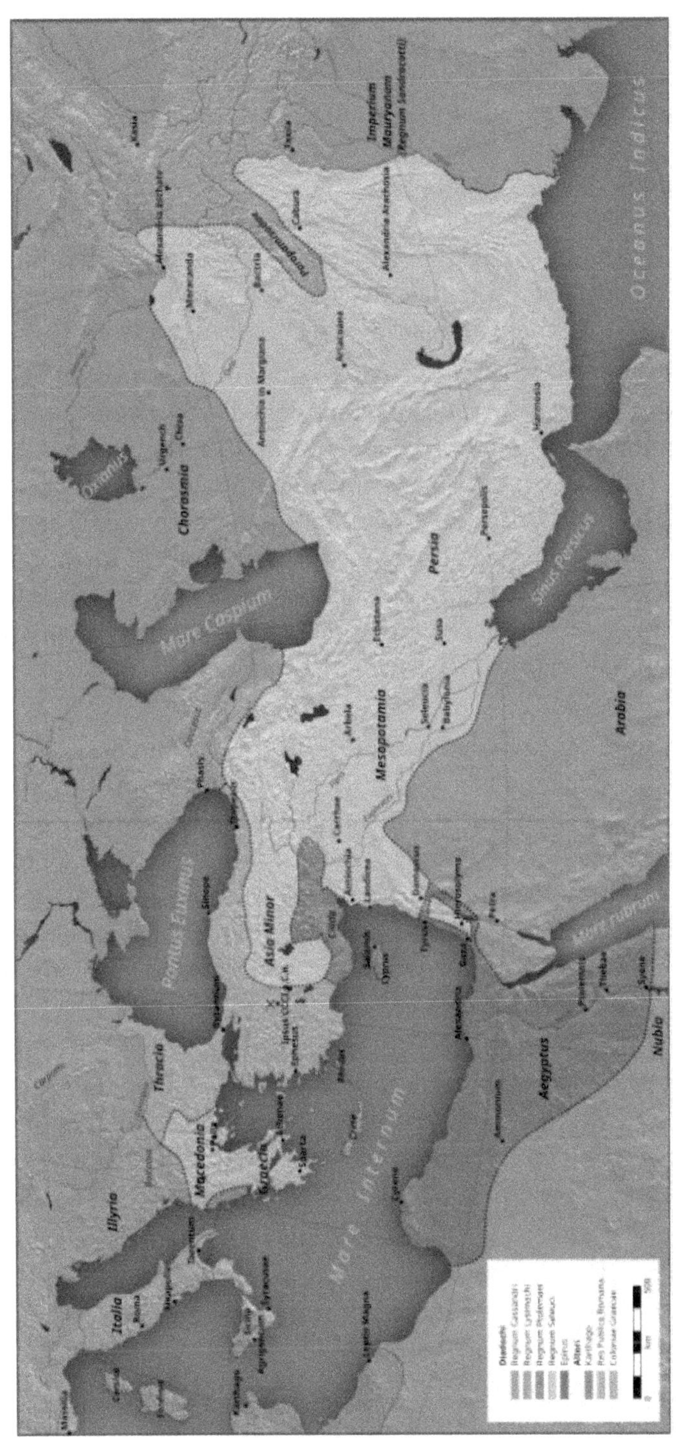

How Alexander's empire was divided.[37]

Egypt went to Ptolemy and his descendants. Ptolemy was the smartest of the Diadochi. He'd grabbed Egypt immediately after Alexander died and successfully secured it from outside attack. Egypt was defensible, incredibly wealthy, and came with Alexandria, the greatest city of the age. The Ptolemies ruled as pharaohs to the Egyptians and Greek kings to the Greeks, getting the best of both worlds. They built a powerful navy, controlled key trade routes, and made Alexandria the cultural capital of the Greek world. The Ptolemaic dynasty lasted nearly three centuries until Cleopatra VII–yes, that Cleopatra–lost everything to Rome in 30 BCE.

Seleucus got the biggest prize geographically: most of Alexander's Asian conquests, from Syria to Afghanistan. It was massive, multicultural, and a nightmare to defend. The Seleucid Empire was too big to hold together. The eastern provinces, including Bactria, Parthia, and others, gradually broke away. Bactria became an independent Greek kingdom in the middle of nowhere. Parthia turned into Rome's great eastern rival. The Seleucids spent centuries watching their empire shrink, focusing more and more on their core territories in Syria and Mesopotamia. They lasted until the 1st century BCE, when Rome and Parthia carved up what remained.

Macedonia–the homeland–went to the Antigonids, descendants of Antigonus's son Demetrius. It was the smallest of the three major kingdoms, but it was maybe the most prestigious. These were Macedonian kings ruling Macedonia, after all. They controlled Greece (sort of–Greek cities never stopped resisting), commanded the strongest army in Greece, and positioned themselves as protectors of Greek culture. However, they never had the wealth of Egypt or the vast territories of the Seleucids. Rome conquered them in 168 BCE.

Smaller kingdoms sprouted across the former empire like mushrooms after rain. Pergamon in western Asia Minor became wealthy and culturally important. Greek kingdoms existed in places Alexander's conquests had touched, spreading Greek culture thousands of miles from Greece. It was messy, violent, and nothing like the unified empire Alexander had built.

The Wars of the Diadochi proved that Alexander's empire had been held together by his personality, his military genius, and the sheer momentum of conquest. Take Alexander away, and the whole thing fell apart. The generals had personal loyalty to Alexander, not to each other or to the idea of an empire. They'd fought together under Alexander, but that didn't mean they liked each other.

The era of politically dominant and independent city-states was definitively over. The future belonged to kingdoms—massive Greek states ruled by Macedonian dynasties. However, the kingdoms the Diadochi built weren't just fragments of Alexander's empire. They were something new. These massive Greek kingdoms combined Macedonian military power with Persian administrative systems and the resources of conquered territories. They were wealthy, cosmopolitan, and culturally vibrant in ways city-states never were. Greek became the international language from Italy to India. Greek culture mixed with local traditions, creating something neither purely Greek nor purely local but something in between.

The last of the original Diadochi, Seleucus, was assassinated in 281 BCE at the age of seventy-seven while gearing up to invade Macedonia. His death marks the conventional end of the Wars of the Diadochi. By then, the Hellenistic world's structure was set. There were three big kingdoms, a bunch of smaller ones, Greek city-states trying (and failing) to stay independent, and Greek culture everywhere. Alexander had wanted to conquer the world. Instead, he transformed it. It was not the legacy he planned, but it may have lasted longer.

The New Age: Hellenistic Culture and Science

The world Alexander created looked nothing like the Greece his father had conquered. Gone were the cozy city-states where everyone knew everyone else's business. In their place rose massive cosmopolitan cities that would have blown an Athenian's mind. Athens and Sparta? They were still there, but now they were provincial backwaters. The real action had moved east to glittering new capitals like Alexandria, Antioch, and Pergamon—cities so vast they made classical Athens look like a village.

Alexandria became the crown jewel. Alexander founded it in 331 BCE on Egypt's Mediterranean coast, and under the Ptolemies, it exploded into perhaps the greatest city of the ancient world. By the 3rd century BCE, perhaps 300,000 to 500,000 people or more lived there—though such figures are speculative—making it one of the largest cities of the era. Greeks, Egyptians, Jews, Syrians, Persians, and Ethiopians all jammed together in a bustling port city. It had a lighthouse so tall (over three hundred feet) that it became one of the Seven Wonders of the Ancient World. It had wide streets, a magnificent harbor, and more money flowing through it than anywhere else in the world.

But the Ptolemies wanted more than just wealth. They wanted Alexandria to be the intellectual capital of the world, so they threw money at scholars like modern tech billionaires throw money at startups. They built the Mouseion, a research institute where scholars lived rent-free and got paid to think. Attached to it was the Great Library of Alexandria, which sought to collect every book ever written.

The Great Library's agents were obsessed. They traveled the Mediterranean, buying manuscripts and copying everything they could find. According to later sources, ships docking in Alexandria were supposedly searched for books. Any books were confiscated and copied. The copies were returned to the owners while the originals went to the Library. Whether this policy was consistently enforced or exaggerated in later retellings, the ambition was clear. At its peak, the Great Library reportedly held somewhere between 400,000 and 700,000 scrolls, though such numbers are estimates based on ancient claims that cannot be verified. It would have essentially been everything the ancient world knew, all in one place.

The result was an intellectual boon that wouldn't be matched for over a thousand years.

Euclid showed up in Alexandria around 300 BCE and wrote a math textbook called the *Elements*. It became *the* geometry textbook for the next two thousand years. Every proof and every theorem you learned in geometry class? That's Euclid. The book was still being used in the 1900s.

Then there was Archimedes, the rock star of ancient science. This man from Syracuse figured out volumes of spheres, discovered the principle of buoyancy, and supposedly ran naked through the streets shouting "Eureka!" after realizing he could measure volume by water displacement while taking a bath. He invented war machines so effective that they held off a Roman siege for years. These giant claws grabbed ships and flipped them over. He came close to inventing methods resembling integral calculus eighteen centuries before Isaac Newton. When Roman soldiers finally took Syracuse and a soldier killed Archimedes (despite orders to capture him alive), the Roman general wept. They had just killed the smartest man in the world.

Eratosthenes looked at shadows and figured out the Earth's circumference. He knew the Earth was round—educated Greeks had known that for ages—and he noticed that at noon on the summer solstice, the sun was directly overhead in Syene (modern Aswan) but cast a shadow in Alexandria. He measured the angle, did some geometry, and calculated the Earth's size. Estimates of his accuracy vary depending on which ancient unit of measurement he used, but he was remarkably close to the actual value.

Aristarchus figured out that the Earth goes around the sun, not the other way around. He was absolutely right, although nobody believed him. Most people, including later astronomers, kept insisting the Earth was the center of everything. It took 1,800 years for Copernicus to revive the heliocentric model, though observational confirmation would come later still. Aristarchus was nearly two millennia ahead of his time.

Medicine got weird and fascinating. Herophilus and Erasistratus dissected human bodies in Alexandria, something Greeks hadn't done before due to cultural taboos about desecrating the dead. They traced nerves, identified parts of the brain, and figured out that arteries carried blood (earlier doctors thought they carried air). Later sources, particularly the Christian writer Tertullian and others often considered hostile to pagan practices, claimed they performed vivisection on living criminals. This charge remains debated among scholars and may reflect anti-Alexandrian propaganda. Regardless, their anatomical work advanced the field by centuries.

All this happened because Hellenistic kings decided that funding science made them look good. The Ptolemies didn't care so much about practical applications. They wanted glory and the greatest minds working in their city. So, they paid scholars to do nothing but research and think. It was perhaps the first time in history that governments systematically funded pure research.

Philosophy changed too, but in a different way. In classical Athens, philosophers asked, "How should we organize society?" In the Hellenistic world, that question was pointless. You lived under a king. You couldn't vote. You couldn't change anything. So, philosophers asked a different question: "How do I stay sane in a world I can't control?"

The Stoics, founded by Zeno around 300 BCE, said one should control oneself since one can't control the world. You can't control things whether you're rich or poor, sick or healthy. But you can control how you react to those things. Accept your fate. Do your duty. Don't get worked up about stuff you can't change. It sounds grim, but it was actually liberating. Stop fighting reality and find peace with what is. The philosophy became enormously influential, eventually spreading to Rome. Even emperors became Stoics.

Epicurus went a different direction. He said pleasure is the goal, but he defined pleasure as not suffering. People should live simply. Don't chase wealth or power. Enjoy friendship. Don't fear death because you won't experience it anyway since you'll be dead. Don't fear gods; they exist, but they don't care about you. It was philosophy for people who just wanted to be left alone and live peacefully.

The Cynics said forget all social conventions. Diogenes reportedly lived in a large ceramic jar or barrel (the exact nature of his dwelling is debated and may be somewhat metaphorical), owned nothing, and mocked everyone. When Alexander the Great visited him and asked what he wanted, Diogenes reportedly told him to stop blocking the sun. The Cynics thought civilization made people miserable and advocated dropping out entirely.

Diogenes by Jean-Léon Gérôme (1824–1904).[28]

These philosophies weren't abstract intellectual exercises. They were survival guides for living in a vast, impersonal world where you had no political power and might not even share a language with your neighbors. While classical philosophy had often focused on civic virtue and political organization, Hellenistic philosophy increasingly emphasized personal ethics and individual tranquility in a world of kingdoms and empires.

Greek culture spread everywhere, but it also changed. In Egypt, Greek gods merged with Egyptian ones. In Bactria (modern Afghanistan), Greek kings ruled for over a century, minting coins with Greek on one side and the local script on the other. Art blended styles. The result wasn't purely Greek or purely local but something new and cosmopolitan.

The Winged Nike made during the Hellenistic age.[39]

The Hellenistic age represented Greek culture's widest expansion and most significant transformation. Classical Greek culture was concentrated and tied to small cities. Hellenistic culture was international, diverse, and mixed with everything it touched. It was less purely "Greek" but influenced far more people across a much wider territory. When Rome eventually absorbed the Hellenistic kingdoms, it inherited this sophisticated Greek culture and spread it even further. The Hellenistic synthesis–Greek learning mixed with Mediterranean and Near Eastern ideas–became the foundation for Roman, Byzantine, and Islamic civilizations. Not bad for a bunch of kingdoms built on the ruins of one man's conquered empire.

The Final Curtain: Greek Kingdoms Meet Roman Power

While the Hellenistic kingdoms fought each other and spread Greek culture across the eastern Mediterranean, a new power was rising in the west. Rome started as one Italian city among many, but by the 3rd century BCE, it had conquered the Italian Peninsula. Then it defeated Carthage in brutal wars that gave Rome control of the western Mediterranean. The Romans were good at war, relentless in pursuit of victory, and willing to grind down enemies through sheer persistence. The Hellenistic kingdoms were about to find out what that meant.

Rome's first major clash with a Hellenistic kingdom was Macedonia. Philip V of Macedon made the fatal mistake of allying with Carthage during Rome's war with Hannibal. Rome didn't forget. After defeating Carthage, Rome turned its attention to Macedonia. The Romans presented themselves as liberating Greece from Macedonian domination, which many Greeks initially welcomed, though for Rome, the outcome was political and strategic dominance.

The decisive battle came at Cynoscephalae in 197 BCE. Philip V commanded a Macedonian phalanx, which had dominated Greek warfare for 150 years. The Roman consul Flamininus commanded legions–flexible infantry that could adapt to terrain and circumstances in ways the rigid phalanx couldn't. The battle was close until Roman maniples (subdivisions of the Roman legion) broke through the Macedonian line and attacked from behind. The Macedonian phalanx, formidable in a head-on clash on level ground, proved vulnerable on rough terrain or when its flanks and rear were exposed. Philip lost and had to accept humiliating peace terms.

Rome announced at the Isthmian Games in 196 BCE that it was granting Greek cities their "freedom." Greeks cheered. They didn't yet understand that Roman "freedom" meant doing what Rome wanted. Any city that resisted found out quickly that Roman patience had limits.

Macedonia tried one more time. Perseus, Philip V's son, built up Macedonia's strength and prepared to challenge Rome. The Third Macedonian War ended at the Battle of Pydna in 168 BCE, where Roman legions destroyed another Macedonian phalanx. This time, Rome didn't just defeat Macedonia; it abolished the kingdom entirely, divided it into four republics, and looted the royal treasury. Perseus was paraded through Rome in chains and died in captivity. The Antigonid dynasty was finished.

When the Greek city of Corinth led a rebellion against Roman domination in 146 BCE, Rome's response was brutal. The Roman consul Mummius besieged Corinth, captured it, killed the men, enslaved the women and children, and burned the city to the ground. Then he looted Corinth's art and treasures and shipped them to Rome. The message was clear: Rome's patience with Greek resistance was exhausted. Greece became a Roman province called Achaea. The classical era of sovereign Greek kingdoms had ended. Greek cities continued to exist, but they were under Roman provincial administration.

The Seleucid Empire lasted longer but suffered a slower death. Antiochus III, called "the Great," tried to expand westward into Greece in the early 2nd century BCE. Rome crushed him at the Battle of Magnesia in 190 BCE and imposed a massive war indemnity that crippled Seleucid finances. The empire began to fragment. Judea rebelled and gained independence. The Parthians conquered the eastern provinces. By the 1st century BCE, the Seleucids controlled only Syria. Rome's intervention in 63 BCE, when Pompey arrived to "settle" affairs in the east, significantly curtailed Seleucid power. Over subsequent decades, the empire fragmented and disappeared. The largest of the Hellenistic kingdoms simply dissolved.

Egypt lasted the longest of the three major Hellenistic kingdoms, surviving until 30 BCE. The Ptolemies were smart. They stayed out of Rome's way, paid tribute, and generally kept their heads down. However, Egypt was too wealthy to ignore forever. By the 1st century BCE, Rome was deeply involved in Egyptian politics, propping up friendly Ptolemies and deposing unfriendly ones.

The end came during Rome's civil wars. Cleopatra VII was the last of the Ptolemies and one of the most capable rulers Egypt ever had. She spoke multiple languages, including Egyptian (unusual among the Greek-speaking Ptolemies), understood economics and politics, and knew Egypt's survival depended on backing the right Roman faction.

She allied with Julius Caesar, had a son with him, and survived Caesar's assassination. Then she allied with Mark Antony, one of the three men who divided the Roman world after Caesar's death. Antony and Cleopatra formed a political and romantic partnership that controlled Rome's eastern provinces. They had children together. They dreamed of an eastern empire centered on Egypt that could rival Rome itself.

It didn't work out. Octavian, Caesar's adopted son and the future Emperor Augustus, painted Antony as a Roman traitor who had been seduced by an eastern temptress. The propaganda worked. At the Battle of Actium in 31 BCE, Octavian's fleet defeated Antony and Cleopatra's combined forces. The lovers fled to Egypt. When Octavian's armies approached Alexandria in 30 BCE, Antony committed suicide. Cleopatra tried negotiating with Octavian but realized she'd either be executed or paraded through Rome as a prisoner. She committed suicide, traditionally said to be by snakebite, though ancient sources differ on the details. The exact method remains uncertain.

Octavian annexed Egypt. The last Hellenistic kingdom became a Roman province. The Ptolemaic dynasty, which had ruled Egypt for nearly three centuries, was gone. The age of Hellenistic kingdoms was over.

Rome conquered the Greek world militarily, but culturally, the opposite happened. The Romans admired Greek culture deeply–maybe too deeply. Wealthy Romans hired Greek tutors for their children. Roman artists copied Greek sculptures. Roman architects imitated Greek temples. Roman writers modeled their works on Greek literature. Latin literature essentially began with translations and adaptations of Greek texts.

The Roman poet Horace summed it up best: "Captive Greece took captive her savage conqueror and brought civilization to rustic Latium." Rome conquered Greece with swords, but Greece conquered Rome with culture. Roman emperors spoke Greek, collected Greek art, and patronized Greek intellectuals. The eastern half of the Roman Empire remained Greek-speaking and culturally Greek. When the Western

Roman Empire fell, the eastern half—the Byzantine Empire—survived for another thousand years as a Greek Christian empire.

The irony is profound. The Greeks lost their political independence. The kingdoms that Alexander's generals built were absorbed by Rome. Greek city-states became Roman municipalities. Greeks could no longer make war or have an independent foreign policy. But Greek language, literature, philosophy, science, and art became a foundational layer of Roman civilization, interacting and blending with Latin, Near Eastern, Egyptian, and local traditions across the Mediterranean and beyond. Christianity, the religion that would dominate Europe and eventually spread globally, developed in a Greek-speaking environment and used Greek philosophical concepts to articulate its theology.

The age of the great Hellenistic kingdoms ended in 30 BCE with Cleopatra's death. However, ancient Greek cultural influence was just beginning its longest and most successful phase, one that continues to this day. The Greeks lost their kingdoms but won the future.

Conclusion
The Legacy of Ancient Greece

Ancient Greece ended over two thousand years ago. The last Hellenistic kingdom fell in 30 BCE. The city-states that invented democracy, the philosophers who asked fundamental questions about existence, the scientists who calculated the Earth's circumference—they're all long gone. Their cities are ruins. Their books survive only as fragments or copies of copies. Most of what they created has been lost to time.

And yet, ancient Greece is everywhere.

You see it every time you vote, every time you go to a theater, every time you think about ethics or logic or politics. Greek words fill English: democracy, philosophy, theater, politics, history, mathematics, physics, and psychology. We use the Greek alphabet in science and math. We name our sports stadiums and government buildings after Greek temples. We argue about ideas that Socrates, Plato, and Aristotle debated 2,400 years ago.

This isn't nostalgia or coincidence. Ancient Greece shaped the foundations of Western civilization so deeply that we often don't even notice.

Start with democracy. Athens invented the idea that ordinary citizens could govern themselves. The Athenian system was flawed. It excluded women, slaves, and foreigners, and it made terrible decisions driven by emotion and politicking. But the core was revolutionary. Political power doesn't have to flow from kings or gods or military might. It can come from the people. That idea died when Rome conquered Greece. It was forgotten for centuries and then revived during the Enlightenment. Modern democracy isn't a copy of Athens; it's representative rather than direct, includes far more people, and has checks against mob rule. However, the inspiration came from Athens. The American Founding Fathers studied Greek history. They knew about Athens's mistakes and tried to avoid them. Without Athens, modern democracy might never have been imagined.

Or philosophy. Before the Greeks, people explained the world through gods and myths. The Greeks were the first to systematically ask "Why?" and demand logical answers. Thales tried to explain nature through natural causes, not divine intervention. Socrates questioned assumptions and demanded definitions. Plato explored justice, knowledge, and reality through reasoned argument. Aristotle categorized everything from ethics to biology to politics using logic. They created the toolkit of Western philosophy. Every Western philosopher since has been responding to Greek ideas, either building on them or arguing against them. Even if you've never read Plato, you live in a world shaped by the assumption that ideas matter, that logic can reveal truth, and that questioning authority is legitimate. That's from ancient Greece.

Science and mathematics owe a similar debt. Pythagoras discovered mathematical relationships in nature. Euclid systematized geometry in a way that's still taught. Archimedes pioneered methods that anticipated calculus. Eratosthenes measured the Earth. Aristarchus proposed heliocentrism. Hippocrates insisted medicine should be based on observation rather than superstition. These weren't just isolated discoveries. They represented a worldview that nature operates by consistent laws that human reason can understand. That assumption underlies all modern science. When scientists today insist on evidence, demand logical consistency, and test hypotheses, they're following a tradition the Greeks started.

Art and literature carry Greek DNA too. Western drama descends directly from Athens. The plays of Aeschylus, Sophocles, Euripides, and Aristophanes established genres, themes, and structures that playwrights still use. Greek epic poetry influenced Roman literature, which influenced medieval literature, which influenced the Renaissance, which shaped everything since. Greek sculpture's emphasis on a realistic human form set standards that dominated Western art for millennia. Even when artists rebelled against classical forms, they were rebelling against Greece.

The influence isn't limited to "the West," whatever that means. When Alexander conquered the Persian Empire, Greek culture spread across the Near East and mixed with local traditions. This Hellenistic synthesis became the foundation for Roman civilization. When Rome split, the eastern half–the Byzantine Empire–remained Greek-speaking and preserved Greek learning for a thousand years. When Islam arose, it encountered this Greek heritage in Syria, Egypt, and Persia. Muslim scholars translated Aristotle, Euclid, and Galen into Arabic, studied them, built on them, and preserved what western Europe had largely forgotten. When medieval Europeans rediscovered Greek philosophy and science, they often learned it through Arabic translations. The Renaissance obsession with reviving classical learning meant studying Greek texts. The Enlightenment's emphasis on reason and natural law drew heavily on Greek philosophy. Every major intellectual movement in Europe for two thousand years defined itself partly by its relationship to ancient Greece.

This isn't to say Greece was perfect or that everything good came from Greece. The Greeks were slave owners who excluded women from public life, waged brutal wars, and committed atrocities. Their philosophers justified slavery. Their democracies could be as tyrannical as any dictatorship. They weren't uniquely rational or enlightened. After all, every culture has its thinkers and achievements. China, India, Persia, and many others developed sophisticated philosophies, mathematics, and governance without any Greek influence.

However, Greece's particular achievements–democracy, systematic philosophy, deductive logic, naturalistic science, and realistic art–spread widely and influenced a lot of people. This was partly due to timing and geography. Greece was positioned between the East and the West. It was close enough to older civilizations to learn from them, but independent enough to develop its own traditions. Alexander's conquests spread Greek culture across a huge area, and Hellenistic kings funded scholars to preserve and expand Greek knowledge. Rome conquered Greece militarily but adopted Greek culture enthusiastically and spread it across its empire. Christianity developed in a Greek-speaking environment and used Greek philosophy to explain theology. It was also partly luck; different choices at key moments could have led to very different outcomes.

The point isn't that ancient Greece was perfect or that it deserves all the credit for Western civilization. The point is that understanding ancient Greece helps us understand ourselves. When we debate democracy's strengths and weaknesses, we're continuing arguments Athenians had. When we wonder about justice, knowledge, or the good life, we're asking Socratic questions. When we insist on evidence, we're using Greek tools. When we watch plays exploring human nature through conflict and tragedy, we're experiencing what Athenians experienced 2,500 years ago.

Ancient Greece also reminds us that civilizations rise and fall but ideas endure. The Greek city-states spent centuries fighting each other, exhausted themselves, and were conquered by outsiders. Their political independence ended. But their ideas—preserved in texts, passed down through generations, and translated into dozens of languages—outlived their empires by millennia. The Greeks lost their kingdoms but won the future in a way no Greek could have imagined.

Walking through the ruins of the Parthenon or the Theatre of Dionysus, it's hard not to feel the weight of time. These were real people arguing in the Assembly, watching plays, debating philosophy, fighting wars, loving, dying, and dreaming about the future. Most of them are completely forgotten. But what they created together—their experiments with democracy, their philosophical inquiries, their scientific discoveries, their artistic achievements—echoes through the centuries. Ancient Greece isn't just history. It's part of who we are and how we think. And that makes it worth understanding, not as some distant or irrelevant period, but as surprisingly, uncomfortably, and fascinatingly alive.

Here's another book by Matt Clayton that you might like

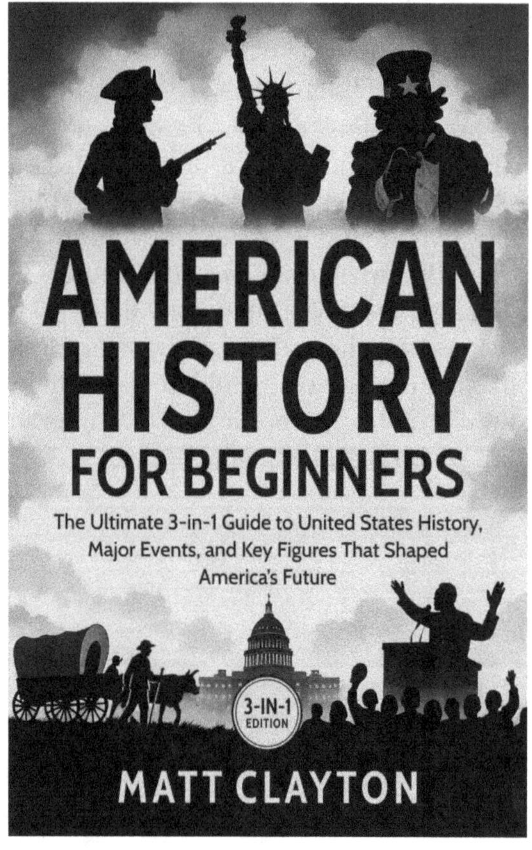

Free Bonus from Captivating History (Available for a Limited time)

Hi History Lovers!

Now you have a chance to join our exclusive history list so you can get your first history ebook for free as well as discounts and a potential to get more history books for free!

Simply visit the link below to join.

captivatinghistory.com/ebook

Or, Scan the QR code!

Also, make sure to follow us on Facebook, X, and YouTube by searching for Captivating History.

Sources

Cartledge, Paul. *Ancient Greek Political Thought in Practice*. Cambridge: Cambridge University Press, 2009.

Cartledge, Paul. *The Greeks: A Portrait of Self and Others*. 2nd ed. Oxford: Oxford University Press, 2002.

Dickinson, Oliver. *The Aegean Bronze Age*. Cambridge: Cambridge University Press, 1994.

Dickinson, Oliver. *The Aegean from Bronze Age to Iron Age*. London: Routledge, 2006.

Martin, Thomas R. *Ancient Greece: From Prehistoric to Hellenistic Times*. 2nd ed. New Haven: Yale University Press, 2013.

Morris, Ian, and Barry B. Powell, eds. *A New Companion to Homer*. Leiden: Brill, 1997.

Osborne, Robin. *Greece in the Making, 1200-479 BC*. 2nd ed. London: Routledge, 2009.

Pomeroy, Sarah B., Stanley M. Burstein, Walter Donlan, and Jennifer Tolbert Roberts. *Ancient Greece: A Political, Social, and Cultural History*. 3rd ed. New York: Oxford University Press, 2012.

Strauss, Barry. *The Battle of Salamis: The Naval Encounter That Saved Greece—and Western Civilization*. New York: Simon & Schuster, 2004.

Lazenby, J. F. *The Defence of Greece, 490-479 B.C.* Warminster: Aris & Phillips, 1993.

Image Sources

1 Bernard Gagnon, CC BY-SA 3.0 <https://creativecommons.org/licenses/by-sa/3.0>, via Wikimedia Commons, https://commons.wikimedia.org/wiki/File:Knossos_-_North_Portico_02.jpg

2 https://commons.wikimedia.org/wiki/File:Knossos_bull_leaping_fresco.jpg

3 User:Alexikoua, User:Panthera tigris tigris, TL User:Reedside, CC BY-SA 3.0 <https://creativecommons.org/licenses/by-sa/3.0>, via Wikimedia Commons, https://commons.wikimedia.org/wiki/File:Mycenaean_World_en.png

4 Joyofmuseums, CC BY-SA 4.0 <https://creativecommons.org/licenses/by-sa/4.0>, via Wikimedia Commons, https://commons.wikimedia.org/wiki/File:Lion_Gate_-_Mycenae_by_Joy_of_Museums.jpg

5 https://commons.wikimedia.org/wiki/File:Athens_%E2%80%94_Mask_of_Agamemnon.jpg

6 https://commons.wikimedia.org/wiki/File:Homer_British_Museum.jpg

7 https://commons.wikimedia.org/wiki/File:Apollon_Tempel_im_antiken_Korinth.jpg

8 Oblomov2, CC0, via Wikimedia Commons, https://commons.wikimedia.org/wiki/File:Vix_crater_hoplite_circa_500_BCE.jpg

9 Dipa1965, CC BY-SA 4.0 <https://creativecommons.org/licenses/by-sa/4.0>, via Wikimedia Commons, https://commons.wikimedia.org/wiki/File:Greek_Colonization_Archaic_Period.svg

10 Sailko, CC BY-SA 3.0 <https://creativecommons.org/licenses/by-sa/3.0>, via Wikimedia Commons, https://commons.wikimedia.org/wiki/File:Ignoto,_c.d._solone,_replica_del_90_dc_ca_da_orig._greco_del_110_ac._ca,_6143.JPG

11 User:Bibi Saint-Pol, CC BY-SA 3.0 <http://creativecommons.org/licenses/by-sa/3.0/>, via Wikimedia Commons, https://commons.wikimedia.org/wiki/File:Map_Greco-Persian_Wars-en.svg

12 https://commons.wikimedia.org/wiki/File:L%C3%A9onidas_aux_Thermopyles_-_Jacques-Louis_David_-_Mus%C3%A9e_du_Louvre_Peintures_INV_3690_;_L_3711.jpg

13 https://commons.wikimedia.org/wiki/File:Battle_of_Thermopylae_and_movements_to_Salamis,_480_BC.gif

14 https://commons.wikimedia.org/wiki/File:Battle_of_salamis.png

15 https://commons.wikimedia.org/wiki/File:Spartans_at_Plataea.jpg

16 https://commons.wikimedia.org/wiki/File:Pericles_Pio-Clementino_Inv269_n2.jpg

17 Steve Swayne, CC BY 2.0 <https://creativecommons.org/licenses/by/2.0>, via Wikimedia Commons, https://commons.wikimedia.org/wiki/File:The_Parthenon_in_Athens.jpg

18 No machine-readable author provided. MatthiasKabel assumed (based on copyright claims)., CC BY-SA 3.0 <http://creativecommons.org/licenses/by-sa/3.0/>, via Wikimedia Commons, https://commons.wikimedia.org/wiki/File:Roman_bronze_copy_of_Myron%E2%80%99s_Discobolos,_2nd_century_CE_(Glyptothek_Munich).jpg

19 Niko Kitsakis, CC BY 4.0 <https://creativecommons.org/licenses/by/4.0>, via Wikimedia Commons, https://commons.wikimedia.org/wiki/File:Varvakeion_Athena.jpg

20 No machine-readable author provided. Harrieta171 assumed (based on copyright claims)., CC BY-SA 3.0 <http://creativecommons.org/licenses/by-sa/3.0/>, via Wikimedia Commons, https://commons.wikimedia.org/wiki/File:Ath%C3%A8nes_Acropole_Caryatides.JPG

21 I, Abu America, CC BY-SA 3.0 <http://creativecommons.org/licenses/by-sa/3.0/>, via Wikimedia Commons, https://commons.wikimedia.org/wiki/File:Greece_alliances_431bc.jpg

22 https://commons.wikimedia.org/wiki/File:Herma_Demosthenes_Glyptothek_Munich_292.jpg

23 https://commons.wikimedia.org/wiki/File:Pelopennesian_War,_Walls_Protecting_the_City,_431_B.C..JPG

24 https://commons.wikimedia.org/wiki/File:Makedonische_phalanx.png

25 https://commons.wikimedia.org/wiki/File:Alexander_and_Bucephalus_-_Battle_of_Issus_mosaic_-_Museo_Archeologico_Nazionale_-_Naples_BW.jpg

26 Generic Mapping Tools, CC BY-SA 3.0 <http://creativecommons.org/licenses/by-sa/3.0/>, via Wikimedia Commons, https://commons.wikimedia.org/wiki/File:MacedonEmpire.jpg

27 Diadochen1.png: Captain_BloodDiadochi IT.svg: Luigi Chiesa (talk) This vector image includes elements that have been taken or adapted from this file: Battle icon

gladii.svg.derivative work: Homo lupustranslator: Manlleus (ca), CC BY-SA 3.0 <https://creativecommons.org/licenses/by-sa/3.0>, via Wikimedia Commons, https://commons.wikimedia.org/wiki/File:Diadochi_LA.svg

28 https://commons.wikimedia.org/wiki/File:Jean-L%C3%A9on_G%C3%A9r%C3%B4me_-_Diogenes_-_Walters_37131.jpg

29 https://commons.wikimedia.org/wiki/File:Nike_of_Samothrake_Louvre_Ma2369_n4.jpg

www.ingramcontent.com/pod-product-compliance
Lightning Source LLC
LaVergne TN
LVHW010034160826
845671LV00004B/200
9781968553296